The *365 Days of Happiness* bestselling author
JACQUELINE PIRTLE

Life IS
Beautiful

Here's to New Beginnings

ISBN-13: 978-1-7320851-6-9

Published by: FreakyHealer

Credits:

Author: Jacqueline Pirtle

Editor in Chief: Zoe Pirtle

Editor/layout: Mitch Pirtle

Book cover design by Kingwood Creations kingwoodcreations.com

Author photo courtesy of Lionel Madiou madiouART.com

Hair styling by Alejandro Jimenez @alejandrojimenezofficial (IG)

DEDICATION

This book is dedicated to Mother Earth, The Heavens, Nature, and Life itself—may humans show nothing but respect, appreciation, gratitude, and love for the gift of being alive in this beautiful physical world.

TABLE OF CONTENTS

ACKNOWLEDGEMENTS

The most incredible creations happen when a beautiful team pulls together!

Thank you for your dedication to make this book tangible.

I give my appreciation to Zoe Pirtle for her editorial mastery; Mitch Pirtle for his editorial and layout love; kingwoodcreations.com for their beautiful and polished book cover design; madiouART.com for an amazing photo shoot; and @alejandrojimenezofficial (IG) for his masterful hair design.

I also would like to give a huge "Thank You!" to all my fans and friends that always urge me to write the next book, and to all who consistently support me.

And from the bottom of my heart... My love goes to my incredible husband, Mitch Pirtle; my phenomenal children, Zoe Pirtle and Till Pirtle; and our sweet cats... Your constant support and belief in me made this new book possible—not to mention the infinite love, laughter, and smiles you are showering me with every single day. Thank you! I love you to the moon and back.

A WORD BY THE AUTHOR

I hope you enjoy this book as much as I loved writing it. If you do, it would be wonderful if you could take a short minute and leave a review on Amazon.com and Goodreads.com as soon as you can. Your kind feedback is much appreciated and so very important for readers to find my work. Thank you!

I also want to let you know that I have published three other bestselling books: *365 Days of Happiness*, a day-by-day guide to being happy; *Parenting Through the Eyes of Lollipops*, a guide for parents to get cracking on conscious/mindful parenting; and *What it Means to BE a Woman*—a heartfelt and empowering book for every woman to experience.

365 Days of Happiness is also available as a companion mobile application for both Android and iPhone and can be supplemented with the appropriate self-study program, consisting of a 7 video course, leading you through the process of reading the book - or following the app - while learning more about being happy. It is a double-win for my *365 Days of Happiness* fans! As a thank you, I am giving all my *365 Days of Happiness* readers this self-study program - worth $29 - for free, as a gift. Simply email my team at info@freakyhealer.com with your receipt of purchase. You can also find out more at www.freakyhealer.com.

All of my books support the teachings of *Life IS Beautiful: Here's to New Beginnings* to help people, parents, and children to BE and live happier - a cause that is very dear to my heart - and are available wherever books are sold, online on amazon.com, amazon websites worldwide, and at www.freakyhealer.com.

For any questions you might have and for more information on what ever else I am up to, visit my website www.freakyhealer.com and my social media accounts @freakyhealer.

WORDS OF WISDOM

Before we start, let me treat you with some wise quotes from the best teachers ever—kids!

"All beautiful things have a connection because they show me love. When I see beautiful birds like the peaceful indigo bunting, it makes life beautiful and that creates love. When I'm snuggled by my kittens, I feel protected from bad spirits. The beauty of life shows love."
~ Hailey Pfeiffer, Age 9

"In a beautiful life you can have so many things, but the truly beautiful thing is yourself."
~ Darcy Lipczenko, age 8

Let these words sink in for a minute!

Then with this clarity in mind, the stage is all yours for you to harmonize with this book and shift towards all beauty and beautiful, and all new beginnings.

LET'S DIVE RIGHT IN

Because why wait…

My name is Jacqueline Pirtle, also known as FreakyHealer.

If you have already read some of my other books, you know that besides being an author I am also a holistic practitioner working with energy; fascinated by energy healing, consciousness, the quantum field, and all metaphysical stuff.

If you have not heard of me yet no hard feelings, promise I won't cry for days—you know me now and can always find out more from my inspirational and happiness provoking life-hack podcast *The Daily Freak*.

I stand powerfully in the pathway of creating what I am called to do with my work and walk the walk of what I speak, write, and teach—otherwise, believe me, I would be all sorts of blocked and stir-crazy in my energetic and physical essences. I invite you to follow your calling and live your life in your own crazy way too, and be prepared for a fast take-off into your high-for-life ways of being and living the wholesomeness of you.

BE and live is one thing that I say often in my work and my books.

With *BE*, I mean existing as your whole being - your energetic essence, body, mind, and consciousness - and how you show up as such.

With *live*, I mean how you are experiencing and animating your physical life—both are explained in more detail in the chapter *Step Six—BE and Live a Beautiful Life*.

High-for-life is something else that I mention all the time. It is a state where you are aligned with your true you, your well-feeling, and your happiness—whatever that might be and no matter the circumstances. Nothing can inspire you to be anyone or anything else than yourself when you are in your high-for-life frequency. It is a constant changing and deeply, securely, rooted-as-yourself, way of being and living. More about this in the chapter *A Star IS Shining High-for-life*.

As a dive-right-into-it option, I invite you to close your eyes and breathe into this by asking yourself what *high-for-life* is for you. Imagine and feel it! Can you *BE* and *live* this for yourself, starting right now?

All my work and books cover different subjects on how to live more mindfully and consciously, however, I always base it on the same pillar-knowing which keeps growing with me as I get older:

Each one of us is an energetic essence, projected into a human body to be and live as a human being in this physical life. Stumbling around in our physicality we seemingly are separate, yet, energetically we are here and connected as one, as one energy and one consciousness. Fact is that what we do, think, say, and who we choose to be, always affects everyone and everything. Fact is also that we are in charge and can choose who we are, how we show up, and how we live this physical experience.

That explains why the connection between my books - me - and you is so vivid even though we are apart—it's our one-ness that always is, never leaves, nor ever ends, that makes it all possible.

This book you are holding in your hands and are compelled to read - or maybe the book has you under its spell and is compelled to be read by you - is about the spiritual and energetic essence of you as a whole being and physical life itself.

It is here to initiate the beauty and all that is beautiful, the pureness and holiness of everything and everyone, all new beginnings, new chances, and new ways to experience a meaningful and conscious physical life existence.

With these written words you will travel down and go way beyond your memory lane—to open and touch your heart, and maybe even shed a healing tear or two. From this moment, you will walk in your life journey supported by your own true story. In beauty and as beautiful, and with the deep conviction that everything and everyone is beautiful too—even the bad and ugly in life, as we call it so mistakenly.

I wrote this book with the intention to initiate a pure finding of yourself by reading, working through, and experiencing what is written. Get ready for a deep mending to happen, because all of this wisdom comes straight from my heart to your heart, my finding-myself to your finding-yourself, my re-remembering to your re-remembering, my re-feeling to your re-feeling, my re-knowing to your re-knowing, and from my deep healing to your deep healing.

In our time together - I think of you reading my book as us spending a splendid time as one - we will touch on the art of living a beautiful life because many of us live on the premises that life is not made of beauty, or it is not as beautiful as it could be. Both false, for sure! There is also the misconception of not being in control of how beautiful we experience life, or the missing belief that beauty and beautiful is indeed the essence of everything and everyone.

With that said, did you arrive on earth misinformed?

No! As newborns, babies, and children, our zest for life, our positive outlook on life and our ability to see, hear, taste, smell, hear, feel, and think of everything and everyone as beautiful, in-awe, in-wonder, and with a constant desire to play is clearly undeniable. You definitely arrived ready for all the fun!

Then where did you pick up this misinformation?

This false tale has been told over and over and has been passed on, generation by generation. Your ancestors chose human reality and reacting to it, over the energetic reality and drawing from that power—as a result, they gave up their control of living their lives fittingly while denying the art of living a beautiful life. Bringing you up as such made your proposed way of living the same—your programming, if you will. More on that in the chapter *It's All in the Perception*.

So where did the belief in the beauty of your energetic essence, your human being, and all of physical life go? Have you forgotten? Is it gone?

Good news, it's definitely not gone, nor forgotten!

So no worries, this on-beauty focused way of being is always there and available for you to shift to. Think of it as being put in a drawer by old life tales that are told and taught over and over—all you have to do is decide to open the drawer without any fear of choosing to be different than others, then instead, choose your deep knowing that the existence of beauty is your truth.

How do you do that?

By re-remembering, re-feeling, and re-knowing that everything and everyone has the potential to be beautiful and by understanding that the only reason why we would think otherwise is because we perceive it as not—hence, we think that the world, life, people, or things are not beautiful.

This brings me to the next topic that we will cover in this book: *The Fake Void*!

Humans think that they don't remember the time when they were just energy, when they were born, and when they were little—creating a fake void that exists only because of one reason.

You are physically alive!

So it only makes sense that letting go of such a silly belief can be very helpful, since, as your energetic essence - where all information that you will ever need is stored - you always remember and always know.

Tempted by the human need to fill this gap and your human desire to know more, people will tell stories about you and your early years. Tales that are purely from their perspectives, since they don't know your views—filling this fake void with the wrong pie filling. Re-remembering and re-knowing guarantees that you will find your right pie filling and can tell your true story—a delicious, completing, and rooting practice indeed.

These realizations make for a powerful initiation to create and nourish your self-knowing and self-understanding—not to mention your true self-feeling and pure self-loving. Big words that are definitely something every human being is wishing for - and more - to feel throughout their physical lifetime.

Let's get busy touching your heart deeply and setting things true for you. These revelations will open your floodgates—so tears of purification, love of a wild and free kind, and all private *else* that is ready to flow, can and will flow.

Oh, and grab a pen, I left you pages throughout the book to write your discoveries down...

Important! Keep in mind to take only what fits for you and leave all else behind because only you know what is best for you—a keystone to practicing the art of living a beautiful life.

Without further ado, let the talks about your special kind of personal re-birth, and how to live life from this new beginning, be the center of your experience. I am really excited for you!

Happiest, Jacqueline

Look around and focus on all beauty. Soon enough, you will believe and know that Life IS indeed beautiful!

NOTHING IS EVER SET IN STONE

Everything can always be changed, shifted, re-directed, stretched, molded, and moved—by you!

Everything is energy—an essence that is holding information, which brings forth the suchlike physical manifestation in physical life. Of course, that is all depending on what reality you choose to experience right at this moment in time.

Since energy is all there is - just think that you are a walking clump of energy - and has been proven as a valid theory by many scientists and physicists, it is only normal to also entertain their theory that multiple dimensions of reality exist, and that consciously or subconsciously you choose the reality you are currently living—making the phrase "You create your own reality!" a very real thing.

I am no scientist or physicist, but I am a professional who researches all universal things deeply—and through personal and work experiences, I chose the theories *everything is pure positive energy at its core* and *I am always in charge to choose my reality* a long time ago. It's where everything and everyone starts and ends because in between, there is our physical experience, lived through our physical bodies and fueled from our energetic essence - the biggest and most intelligent part of us - that is always ONE with consciousness.

"Why even bother with physicality?" You might ask.

Well, besides tasting delicious cake, chocolate, and red wine, physicality is clearly an energetic choice we made - to come forth into this physical life and be exposed to physical manifestations and life happenings - in order to expand and calibrate as our energetic essence and the one-ness we all are. I think that way of being here is phenomenal and choose the awesomeness of this reality each time anew—a wonderful ritual and way to be.

I also understand that there are different opinions about life, and like with everything else, different people are polarized to different beliefs. This is fascinating because diversity is an interesting creator-tool for everyone and everything—to expand and calibrate towards what one likes or wants to be. Just think if all would be the same, no expansions or new creations would exist—same old, same old, while never being challenged to figure out anything new.

So let's agree that:

• Energy is the building block of all that shows itself in physical manifestation - a human or car - and in physical life—feelings, words, moments, happenings, and thoughts.

• Energy is an entity that is constantly moving, new, and always changing—since everything and everyone is energy on the smallest level, it is only natural that everything and everyone is always new and changing. Never set in stone!

• You are in charge of your energy - reality - and can change at anytime

What does that mean?

The essence of all - you and your life too - is a changeable matter and, actually, rather famous for its flexibility, changeability, and shift-ability—clarifying deeply that you are never stuck, even if it seems that way.

Staying always the same and wishing for physical life to stand still - even for just a moment - is against all possibilities and robs you of being connected, let alone listening to your inner voice accurately and according to its speed, creating hardship with real physical life exhaustion. No one has to live and stay that way, no one said that is what they will naturally choose over and over as a life experience, and no one is ever made to stay that way.

You can choose and change your own reality anew at any moment—the result being, you can always change the way you feel according to what is nicest for you. You get to choose *what* and *how* you want to be at any split second!

As a great example, let's choose beauty and beautiful:

Beauty and beautiful is not *who* you are and it has nothing to do with how big or small, tall or short, or fit and unfit you are. Beauty and beautiful only has to do with how you feel and think about yourself, and how you carry yourself; explaining clearly that beauty and beautiful is an energetic essence—flexible, changeable, and shift-able by you and according to the reality you choose. Then, as that chosen reality, it shows itself in your physical life and your physical manifestation of who you are. The result, you feel and think beautiful about yourself. You show up as your undeniable beauty. Your surroundings experience you as your beautiful essence and beautiful physical manifestation—hence people are gushing, "You are so beautiful!" or "You are such a glowing beauty/handsomeness!"

Fact is, in order to be and stay beautiful - youthful, successful, abundant, or anything really - you must choose to feel, think, show up, and act like it—resulting in a shift in your energy that creates the matching essence for you to BE and live as such in your physical life.

Here is one of a million great exercises to play and practice with your energy, your choosing, your creation of essence, and your manifestation skills:

To bend your feelings into alignment, focus on choosing clearly *what* energetic essence you want yourself to be. For instance, do you want to be connected, rooted, grounded, or free?

Choose by asking and feeling yourself into what essence is right for you right now. Shift by practicing the aligned essence in a fitting way—meditation, physical movement, time spent in nature, feel good hobbies, or education. Then BE and live connected, rooted, grounded, or free to experience life as you want it to be—and watch your surroundings change accordingly.

For example:

• Ask yourself if being connected is best for you! If the answer is yes, working on connecting to the Heavens, Mother Earth, Nature, and your Soul Being is key since you either lost your connection or never had it. This makes for situations where you can't clearly decide something, because you can't hear your inner voice guiding you towards what is right for you. "I can't decide," or "I don't know," are clear sayings that fall into this category. If by any chance you can't decide because it's simply not the right time, your inner guidance will let you know once you are connected.

• Ask yourself if being rooted is best for you! This makes sense in situations where life is shaky and uncertain—fear, distrust, and an inability to grow are clear signs of this. Working on rooting yourself into steadiness makes sense for this experience since rooting anchors you until you wont leave your center anymore.

• Ask yourself if being grounded is best for you! Situations where you feel nervous, anxious, unable to relax, or like you are floating out in space - somewhat lost - are longings for a deep grounding to bring yourself down to earth, since floating out in the universe does not feel good at the moment.

• Ask yourself if being completely free and unattached is best for you! When life asks you to be flexible, free, unattached, and wild - maybe even crazy - because in that craziness lays all that you have ever wanted, then it is time for you to BE and live free. Being connected, rooted, and grounded would not be helpful here since they are sometimes a great habitat for us to play it safe - especially with old habits and beliefs - and keep adventures away. Going the being-free route for a little bit will re-write those old ways, and allow vividness and fun to become your normal.

There are so many ways for you to bend and dance with your energetic you, and as an echo, with your physical you.

Face it! You are a world-class chooser, a universal-class creator, and an earth-class manifest-er! Get over it already, claim that power!

So how do you choose your reality wisely and in alignment—for you to feel well and happy?

This is where your energetic essence, your soul being, your spiritual you, your highest good, your inner being, your intuition - however you like to call it - comes in. It is the biggest part of you, one that you were even before being human, that you consistently are; and that you will be, even after transitioning from physical back to energetic.

Imagine this. Think of a wonderful thought leader that you admire, trust, listen to, honor deeply, look up to, and resonate 100% with!

Your inner you is that thought leader! Actually, it is even better because no thought leader out there will ever know more about you - let alone what is better for you - than your own soul being that has been around for a long time, is with you right now, and always will be expanding and calibrating for you. Being connected to this beautiful part of you means that you are joined at the hip with your deepest and most accurate knowing there is. It is the grandest part of you, has answers that are uniquely fitted for you, the intelligence you are always seeking, and all that you will ever need in order to do well and phenomenally in your life.

Plus, whereas it is only natural to outgrow any thought leader at some point - as you change your resonation changes too - you will never feel the need to cut cords with your inner being, because your soul is you. It's a perfect team-match made in heaven and always caught up. If trouble in paradise ever arises, know that it is your physical you that is not keeping up with your inner guidance, never the other way around.

Here are some great ways to connect to your inner intelligence:

- Go inward, meditate, become still, and BE in your heart.

- Learn more about yourself by taking a deep interest in how you feel.

- Follow your well-feeling, your bliss, your happiness, and your heart.

- Take excellent care of your emotional, energetic, and physical wellbeing.

- Pay attention to your inner knowing that is showing up in words, visions, feelings, images, sounds, smells, or happenings—even if in your mind you have no idea where it is coming from. Your heart knows that this guidance is right for you. Give this wisdom the attention and trust it deserves by honoring it and listening. The hint is that if it feels heavenly good to receive, it's yours to follow and nourish.

- Ask questions like: What am I doing with my intuition? Do I hear it—am I connected? Do I shush it away as crazy thinking? Do I trust it? Do I believe it? Do I put it aside for later? Do I trash it away like garbage? Do I use my busy-ness as an excuse to not have to deal with it? Do I follow it blindly? If any of your answers are of a denying nature, you got some connection work to do. Get excited, this book is your solution!

I urge you to realize that your inner knowing is *you* talking to *you*—nobody else's business is ever involved in this pure good-feeling wisdom.

How do you know that it is only *you* talking to *you*?

Easy! If it feels good it is purely you! If the slightest - or mountainous - amount of unwell-feeling is accompanying your knowing, it is not just you. That is the time when you go inward and clean the impurity with meditation, deep breathing, dancing, vivid exercise, a good laugh or two, and try again when it is only *you*—when *you* feel good again.

You inner being will always want the absolute best for you. *You* can trust *you!* *You* can follow *you* blindly! You can with absolute sure-ness and without any questioning always go with what *you* is guiding *you* to do.

Between everything always being shift-able, and your inner knowing guiding you towards choosing a new and better reality for yourself at any given moment, you are very set to live your physical life in a beautiful style.

If you choose to live this way, you are going with the natural flow of what you came here to experience—a reality in which nothing is ever wrong, and even better, where you can choose new and change at any moment.

It is a beautiful life indeed—so let's get rooted in it...

Look around and focus on all beauty. Soon enough, you will believe and know that Life IS indeed beautiful!

IT'S ALL IN THE PERCEPTION

The sayings of the past...

Think of what you heard while growing up:

Life is not fair.

Life is hard.

Life is full of problems.

What will others think?

Behave, comply, and say yes!

Being angry or fighting is wrong.

That person did this to me.

This is because of this/that.

Fear is real.

Suffering is real and normal.

You have to work hard or you won't get anywhere.

Doing nothing does not get you anywhere.

Do better! Do more!

What is wrong with you?

Being sick sucks!

Money does not grow on trees.

Money is evil.

You get the energetic sense of these sayings. They are all about pressure, resistance, hardship, anger, frustration, negativity, and being stuck and powerless in a life with limitless obstacles.

Now imagine that all of these sayings above are replaced with the words below:

Life is beautiful!

Don't worry!

Slow down!

Connect to your inner voice—you have all the answers.

Choose well-feeling, happiness, and bliss over anything.

Does this feel good to you—follow your heart!

You know best for yourself—you are in charge!

This obstacle is beautiful, it initiates change!

Refusing all non-fitting means you're aligning with you.

Fighting and being angry while in alignment is beautiful.

Having no money initiates a money-relationship healing.

There is always a way forward!

Things always change—you can *create* change.

Losing my job helped me find myself.

Being sick teaches me to listen to my physical body.

Experiencing fear makes me focus on growing my trust.

You never lose someone—transition is all there is.

Transitioning = shifting into energetic wholesomeness.

Energetic wholesomeness = a space where all is ONE.

This situation might not be as we want it to be, that is okay.

Everything and everyone is beautiful as is.

You can change everything to be more beautiful.

You choose and create your own reality!

Close your eyes and sense the energy of these empowering, positive, peaceful, hopeful, and beautiful words! Breathe in their value. If that is what you would have heard while growing up and were saying to yourself all along, do you think you would live your life differently?

I think so, and know it is so, for me.

Think how your connection and relationship to beauty and beautiful would be today if you naturally knew and understood that there is beauty in everything and everyone—also in anger, sadness, fear, pain, disaster, chaos, and loss; in every aspect of life!

Imagine how healthy your physical body and mind, and how strong your connection to your inner guidance, would be. Your life would be nothing short of magical if these words and their wonderful value would have been your nourishment while growing up—same goes for your ancestors.

Guess how in response you would create more and more of that positive deliciousness, since you create your next from how you feel and think right now. Your life would be naturally experienced and created through a never-ending stream of epic-ness.

Hearing and witnessing over and over that things are hard, ugly, and negative - and that beauty is missing - you believed it over and over—made it your truth. This is not to say that anyone did you wrong. Not at all! Instead, there is unlimited beauty in this because you gained a life maturity through which you can now make fitting choices, the first most important one being, to let this negativity passing-on be as is and embrace it as an old untruth that helped you find your own preference of choosing beauty in the midst of ugliness.

You have a real chance to re-write everything by starting to talk to yourself, everything and everyone, and especially your children about how beauty is all there is; that even in the darkest moments in life, beauty is always there if we choose to focus on it.

Think of what this does for yourself, everyone around you, and your children:

- By reprogramming yourself to BE and live in beauty, you will be beautiful in every aspect of your whole being and will treat your children and loved ones as such too.

- By witnessing you, your loved ones - especially your children - will naturally know and understand that the essence of beauty is the root of everything and everyone. They will spread and share this beautiful way of being to everything and everyone, including their children, and so on. Voila, a new way of living is created. By you!

It is all in the perception of how you believe that something is, which is different for everyone—just think that some feel red as aggressive whereas others sense red as beautiful. Result being, that we are in charge of choosing our beliefs and absolutely capable of dismantling the old and made-up tales that others tell; about how they experience life, and how they say life works.

You are in charge of yourself, your life, and how you experience being here!

So let's get to work…

Look around and focus on all beauty. Soon enough, you will believe and know that Life IS indeed beautiful!

BEAUTY AND BEAUTIFUL

Beauty and beautiful is always whatever you want it to be!

The range of what beauty and beautiful means is yours to choose, and can go anywhere from vacationing at the most beautiful place on earth, to wearing the most beautiful outfit ever; or being over the moon about a clean toilet, since it is sheer beauty to sit your bottom onto something that is so squeaky clean.

You are in total charge of your personal relationship to beauty and beautiful!

As we covered in the chapter **Nothing is Ever Set in Stone**, everything and everyone is energy first and foremost—so are words, feelings, opinions, expectations, and happenings. Everything!

As words, beauty and beautiful carry the energy of special, happiness, bliss, health, nature, betterment, positivity, luxury, glamour, easiness, abundance, wonderful to the eye and heart, a sort of supposed to be like that and naturally as is—and all else that you make it to be.

Seeing, hearing, tasting, smelling, and thinking of - plus feeling - beauty and beautiful is a pure alignment with the untouched natural energetic and physical world, and what it has to offer. This is the natural way of things, until humans strip it away with their actions, ways, and disalignment—then declaring it to be the opposite, ugliness.

Just think of nature and its bountiful wonders. There is nothing but beauty present—even when animals are hunting other animals, the natural beauty of a nourishing value and pure survival is printed in this happening.

This makes for a great case to recondition and align yourself towards beauty all the time, since beauty and beautiful is always there. To think that beauty exists, to hear beauty everywhere, to see the beauty in all, to taste and smell beautifully often, and to feel that beauty is always present in, on, and around you is a powerful clarity—because beauty is inevitable. So why not save your precious energy of the human-proving-it-wrong action to uglify life and instead trust that fact, knowing, and delicious feeling fully and vividly?

Beauty and beautiful is unavoidable and in order to escape it you have to put an enormous effort into dodging and not experiencing it. That effort is exhausting and creates sadness, anger, frustration, and an unlimited amount of unwell-feelings. You might even feel that life is nothing like you want it to be, that none of your desires and wishes are reachable, let alone coming into realization. It's a dilemma that keeps feeding itself by focusing on a reality in which the existence of beauty is denied.

That disallowance is wide spread! Just see how many people are swimming and floating in the fed up masses that have no regard or intention to shift the focus to the beauty on this earth, to the beauty of being alive, to the beauty of our multidimensional beings and universe, and to the beauty of consciousness.

It is easy to latch onto a mob-movement since it is our most conditioned way to confine with the mass-normal. For most people, their unique and deep understanding, knowing, and trusting that life is actually more beautiful than the opposite, was never tickled into aliveness or nourished because of their upbringing, the upbringing of their parents, and that of their grandparents. Their focus on experiencing beauty stayed un-trained or was never fully trained... Notice how I use the word *trained*.

Yes, you can train and re-train your focus and it's actually easy-peasy, if I might say.

But like every beautiful pie, there are certain steps you have to take in order to make it beautiful and tasty. Experiencing a beautiful life that is focused on beauty is no different! There are steps that you have to take. The result being, a guaranteed deliciously enjoyable time.

There is so much freedom to create your flavor of beauty and beautiful! So roll up your sleeves and enjoy the following six steps of beautification—for yourself and your life...

Look around and focus on all beauty. Soon enough, you will believe and know that Life IS indeed beautiful!

SIX STEPS TO LIVE A BEAUTIFUL LIFE

Living and experiencing the beauty of life is what's on the main menu of being alive—it's what you came here to do and chose to master.

Does that mean there is only one way to live life?

No, of course not! But it does mean that whatever you choose in your life and however you choose to live your life is representing your expectations and beliefs of what a beautiful life is—because you are the only one who sets the tone of what beautiful and beauty is for you.

Notice the word *choose*, because even if not consciously, you are still choosing subconsciously. Either you choose consciously to take matters in your own hands and align with your beautiful life or you automatically live life as you have been conditioned and programmed—subconsciously.

It is always a choice and you are always in charge, and it can be changed as soon as you choose to take full responsibility for how you think, feel, see, hear, taste, smell, behave, and live your essence as a whole being in your physical life.

If you are happy, then your choice of beauty is happiness. If you are suffering, then your choice of beauty is sufferance, but not to worry, because both - happiness and suffering - are energies and equally beautiful with endless beauty included; always changeable and shiftable. The only difference in the two is how you think and feel about them, and even that you can change at any time. So no matter your circumstances, the only question on point is, "Am I experiencing my life as beautiful?" and never, "Is what's happening to me beautiful?"

If your answer is "Yes! I am having a beautiful blast!" keep living and striving for the experience of beauty and beautiful in everything that is there for you—the good, the bad, and the ugly. And certainly, continue the fantastic work of strengthening your senses and your connection to living even more high-for-life, since there is never a ceiling to how wonderful life can be. Enjoy the following *Six Steps to Live a Beautiful Life*, which will help you with that. Your alignment with beauty really suits you!

If your answer is "*No!*"—keep your socks on. I got you covered! The following *Six Steps to Live a Beautiful Life*, and what you learn about yourself in the process, will get you there. It will blow your mind how fast you grow your confidence into the ballpark of believing that your life is beautiful. To be honest, I can't wait for you to watch in delight how heads will turn in admiration and how people will hunt you down, just to ask what magic you got going.

Are you ready to mold your life towards bliss? Then grab your pen and let's go…

Look around and focus on all beauty. Soon enough, you will believe and know that Life IS indeed beautiful!

STEP ONE: CHOOSE A BEAUTIFUL LIFE

Nothing ever goes on without a choice being made first—no cake is baked without someone choosing to bake it, no bed is made without someone choosing to make it, and no life is lived without someone choosing to live it.

To choose a beautiful life means that at some point during your time in physicality, you have to take action that stems from your committed attitude of, "That's it!"

- I choose to BE and live, see, hear, taste, smell, think, and feel that life is beautiful

- I believe that there is always beauty in everything and everyone—no matter the circumstances

- I align with my birthright—a life that is outfitted with as much beauty and bliss as I want

The flavor of that once-in-a-lifetime choice needs to be serious and without any possibility to ever cancel. You have to treat it like a real contract between you and your life—one that it is so set and secure that if needed, you would defend it with your own life.

Sounds pretty serious, but isn't living a beautiful life worth standing for to no end since aligning with beauty is what life is all about?

Think of the choices in your life that you have made so far:

The ones that you made loosey-goosey are probably not of value - or even a thing - anymore. Choosing a beautiful life only once in a while, when it is easy, or exclusively when it is already beautiful, is loosey-goosey. This type of choosing will only hold up for a little bit and will not give you the master beauty that it could be.

Now think of the ones that you made with a seriously committed attitude while choosing this or that for real—those are the ones that lead you somewhere further, and higher, in life. Choosing a beautiful life no matter the circumstances, people, or anything really, is when life will show you its grace to the fullest and when beauty and bliss is long-lasting. Even in moments when you get off track, this powerful choice will hold you steadily rooted in a deep knowing, remembering, and understanding of how to latch onto your choice again—or what your choice was in the first place.

Positioning strongly as such also means that what you are saying is, "I am done with the un-beautiful attitude and ways of mine!" Can't get any more beautiful than that since you taking responsibility for how you live your life is your gate to all the happiness, beauty, bliss, health, love, fun, and abundance that you could wish for.

Choosing a beautiful life is a matter of making it your normal way of living—and that takes determination, bravery, and sometimes real, hard, focused, sweat-work. But…

• For one, when the exchange is happiness it does not count as hard work; rather, it's happy work.

• For two, focusing is really good for your brain and mind to stay hard-headed—a great life skill to have.

• For three, sweating is proven to be healthy for your physical body.

Keep in mind that this is a choice that at first is strictly serious but then carried-out lightheartedly ever after—to become the space in which you can experience beauty, enjoyment, and satisfaction.

One might say that this "choosing business" equals a perfectly healthy lifestyle!

Going into this life journey knowing that the first step is a choice, makes it easier for you to handle all ups, downs, lefts, and rights that cross your path. Just say, "Oops, I got carried away, better get back to mastering my beautiful life like a champion!" and go back to your initial choice—to align with beauty and the art of living a beautiful life.

To make this serious and stick, fill out the contract I prepared for you on the next page. Use your own words and elaborate about your choice, then sign it with a celebratory moment of stillness and deep breathing. Don't forget to smile! Place the contract where you can see and reach it easily to re-read and re-choose when needed. That's especially helpful in the beginning of your new chosen lifestyle. As an idea and for focus and determination purposes, put a picture of the contract as your screen saver.

Important! Update and reword your contract often—to keep up and aligned with your ever-so-beautiful changing you.

To create a beautiful life, it takes your conscious choice!

Look around and focus on all beauty. Soon enough, you will believe and know that Life IS indeed beautiful!

CONTRACT

BETWEEN ME AND MY BEAUTIFUL LIFE

Name :

Date :

I hereby promise to give my absolute best in choosing to BE and live, see, hear, taste, smell, think, and feel that *Life IS Beautiful.*

I hereby promise to give my absolute best to believe that there is always beauty in everything and everyone—no matter the circumstance.

I hereby promise to give my absolute best in aligning with my birthright—a life that is outfitted with as much beauty and bliss as I want.

I will do the promised through the following ways, practices, and priorities:

_____

_____

_____

_____

_____

_____

_____

_____

_____

_____

_____

_____

_____

_____

_____

_____

_____

_____

_____

_____

_____

Sign here:

STEP TWO: COMMIT TO A BEAUTIFUL LIFE

Try to make something committed unhappen! Not possible, or at the least, no easy task!

What is a commitment?

Commitment vibrates in a powerful frequency and carries the energetic information - remember everything is energy, carrying information, as covered in the chapter **Nothing is Ever Set in Stone** - of, "I really want this; I will do that; I will make it happen; I say yes!"

Commitment is also a strong act in physical life. Someone committing has the value of, "I give it everything I got!"

I can feel this powerful energy just by thinking and writing about it, without even making a commitment—that is how mighty the frequency of commitment is.

Your committing is based on a powerful willingness and a strong-stamina infused energy that is in you. It is you! It grows from something that captured your eye and is very dear to your heart, which is then nourished by you following said passion, making you feel wonderful in the process.

Of course there are also loosey-goosey ways to commit, but as we covered in the chapter **Step One—Choose a Beautiful Life**, not much long lasting-ness and sturdiness comes out of that sort of dedication. And to be honest, since *commitment* carries the energy of, "I seriously mean it," why would you want to waste any of this powerful value on something that you don't really mean or can't commit to? That screams clear disalignment and a diverted direction from who you really are, since alignment is what you are seeking.

I invite you to seriously and consciously become aware of all your commitments, big or small, and when you make them. Are you really meaning it? Are you squeezing the most out of the value of committing? Are you feeling aligned with the powerful frequency of committing and the commitments that you are making?

If your answer is "Yes!" then keep committing! If it's "No!" adjust and truthfully commit to what is really committable for you right now. Only *real* committing is in alignment and powerful!

The following pages are reserved for you to get real with yourself and create your personal list to commit to living a beautiful life. Write down all that catches your eye, is dear to your heart, and that is a clear passion—be it meditation, movement, laughter, art, music, healthier food, exercise, or letting people off the hook.

Important! Please keep adding on, changing, and updating when needed. Re-read what your commitments are - or even better put them on your phone - to avoid forgetting what your are committing to!

To create a beautiful life, it takes your conscious choice and your serious commitment!

Look around and focus on all beauty. Soon enough, you will believe and know that Life IS indeed beautiful!

_____

_____

_____

_____

_____

_____

_____

_____

_____

_____

_____

_____

_____

_____

_____

_____

_____

_____

_____

STEP THREE: PRACTICE A BEAUTIFUL LIFE

Practice makes perfect!

I used to hear that phrase a lot when I was younger, and even though I did not always like it - for instance with math - it did bear fruit but only if I chose and committed first. Without these first two steps, practicing never did the trick—hence, math frustration took over.

It is the same with living a beautiful life. Nobody can choose or commit to it for you, it is solely up to you, and without seriously choosing and committing first, practicing will lose its flair fast.

The good news is that you can choose and commit at any age, re-choose and re-commit in every split second of your life, and change and shift with speed—making practicing always possible and proving that the universe really does love you, because it is making it easy for you!

How does practicing the art of living a beautiful life look like?

There are many different ways:

Of course there is the enjoyment of the beauty of your energetic being, your soul being, your eternal essence, your higher good, the biggest part of you—whatever you like to call it. It is beautiful, infinite, pure, has all the answers and is always right. You might as well give it the throne!

Then there are your other energetic parts that want to party with you; your mind, your feelings, and your one-ness with consciousness. Your mind has the beautiful capability to think wonderful thoughts—think them! Your feelings have the beautiful ability to create happiness; a happy life is a beautiful life! You being one with all lets you latch onto everything and everyone that is of well-feeling nature, no matter if near or far. That beautiful capability lets you multiply the goodness by the millions through sharing and spreading the joy. Be generous!

Plus, there is the incredible focus on your wonderful physical body—how beautifully it works for you, how organized it is, how automatically it runs, how it always lets you know what's going on - clearly, truthfully, and immediately - and how it never lies but always has your back. Love your body!

Another way to practice, is by looking around in physical life and focusing on the beauty that is presented to you and for you. Enjoy the sky, birds, flowers, rain, people, places, colors, and things. All of it!

Practicing also includes talking about beauty to yourself and others. Mentioning beautiful things in and on you - and in and on others - means that you are showering yourself and others with beautiful words and compliments—with beautiful energy. Just think how saying, "This is a flower!" versus "This is a *beautiful* flower," is millions in worth apart. It's a potent way of practicing the artful way of living a beautiful life.

Being mindful about all beauty is key to practicing successfully. Without your focus on seeing, hearing, tasting, smelling, feeling, and thinking of all beauty, there really is no conscious practice taking place—the result being that your desired change in life is not as huge as it could be.

With practice comes automation - sometimes over time, but it can also be as fast as a race car - in which you naturally will be pulled to focus on seeing, hearing, tasting, feeling, smelling, and thinking only of all beauty. That is where "practice makes perfect" has its say!

Once in a while you will still stray from that beauty-automation. This is normal! Take these moments as great practice to fortify and strengthen your natural pull towards all beauty. Acknowledge your straying and accept, respect, appreciate, thank, and love these moments as the beautiful gifts they are—pockets to re-focus on your choice and commitment. Then get back to practicing bliss.

The next few pages are for you to note the great fitting practices that you have up your sleeve and will perform all the time.

Important! Add on and come up with new ways often— keep the list growing to align yourself as you live your life. When re-visiting your list, focus on feeling yourself being pulled into experiencing the beauty of your life, again and again.

To create a beautiful life, it takes your conscious choice and your serious commitment that is followed by your mindful practice.

Look around and focus on all beauty. Soon enough, you will believe and know that Life IS indeed beautiful!

_____

_____

_____

_____

_____

_____

_____

_____

_____

_____

_____

_____

_____

_____

_____

_____

_____

_____

_____

_____

_____

_____

_____

_____

_____

_____

_____

_____

_____

_____

_____

_____

_____

_____

_____

_____

_____

_____

_____

_____

_____

_____

_____

_____

_____

_____

_____

_____

_____

_____

_____

_____

_____

_____

_____

_____

_____

_____

_____

STEP FOUR: GROW A PASSION

Being passionate about the art of living a beautiful life,
means that you are one of the greatest artists alive!

Passion is the infinitely vivid energetic frequency of being in
the flow and getting lost in bliss. It is a space in which you
forget yourself, time, place, and sometimes even your name.
Being passionate also means that you are bold and beautiful—
you might even add wild to this mix.

Experiencing passion is magical, healing, and of a very
creative nature—no negativity, anger, fright, or suffering is
present when you live passionately. Just think when you
passionately stand *for* something - for the love of something -
the opposite has no presence in your passion.

Passion enables you to go, do, act, be, and live without
limits because it is a heart produced feeling—since your heart
is the host of your limitless soul and is fed its wisdom by your
soul intelligence, anything that is produced in your heart, love
too, is limitless.

When you are passionate, old beliefs and gunky habits have
no oxygen to survive; instead, laughter, playfulness, deep
knowing, and good-for-you careless-ness takes over. Others
might even think that you have lost it or are completely nuts—
a scenario showing that you have arrived at the top of passion,
the top of living a vividly successful and beautiful life, and the
top of being you. Bravo, you made it!

How do you grow passion for living a beautiful life?

By choosing, committing, and then practicing what you are
wishing to experience, you will give birth to your passion. It's a
given! It is also common sense that the more steady you
practice, the bigger and more humongous your passion will
grow—hopefully, all the way until you being passionate about

living a beautiful life becomes your normal; until it becomes who you are, and the best about that is, since you are an ever calibrating being, your passion will always calibrate naturally with you.

Of course, passion is always birthed best from a lighthearted and blissful space—never from a "have to," "need to," or "should" way of living. Just imagine a passionate painter that "has to" paint the next painting. It won't work, or at least not as beautifully as it could.

If you ever do get off your bliss-path, you will know instantly because you will feel your passion being gone—leaving a nice big hole behind that in order to feel wonderful again, will need to be filled with urgency. Promise, you will know!

How do you tickle your passion into being-ness again?

By re-remembering what you chose and committed to in the first place and getting your beautiful behind back to practicing, you will be back in your bliss-action in no time. Your passion will be there for you, waiting with a passionately tapping foot, wondering where the *bleep* you went—because for clarity's sake, your passion never left. That is when you have found your artful way again, and onward you go you passion crazy you!

I invite you to go ahead and close your eyes. Breathe a few times in and out. When you are relaxed and can sense yourself being in a sort of nothing space, visualize yourself as a passionate human being. Choose whatever makes you feel the wildest and boldest in your passion—keep imagining and feeling this incredibly vivid version of you. Fill every single cell of yours with this creative fierceness, aliveness, and excitement.

How does this look, feel, taste, smell, or sound? What are your thoughts? Are you envisioning that you are passionate about your energy, love, art, life, children, family, or food?

When satisfied, describe what you just felt and imagined over the next few pages. Use distinctive words and phrases that represent your feelings on passion, being passionate, and your passion for being and living your beautiful life.

Important! Add on and change these writings often because you want to keep up with your always expanding passionate you.

To create a beautiful life, it takes your conscious choice and your serious commitment that is followed by your mindful practice; which creates your passion.

Look around and focus on all beauty. Soon enough, you will believe and know that Life IS indeed beautiful!

STEP FIVE: IT'S A DEVOTION, NURTURE IT!

Being devoted means you can't live without "it" anymore, or that you can't live any other way from this point forward.

Living a beautiful life and experiencing all the beauty there is should be that "it" that you can't live without anymore, let alone ever settle for less.

A devotion means that you are giving yourself fully to something. You lay right into it with complete trust and clear knowing that this is the right thing for you to do, follow, choose, commit, practice, and be passionate about.

Devotion has the energetic value of purity, clarity, celebration, highness, meaningfull-ness, beauty, and beautiful. Saying, "I devote myself and my life to this!" is of highest value. Are you feeling the happy goose bumps yet?

I truly hope that after reading, practicing, and writing about step one through four, you are either getting close to being devoted to the art of living a beautiful life or are already there—both being a clear sign that you are really getting the hang of losing yourself in bliss. Bravo and stay on it!

If not, keep reading and practicing; your devotion is just around the corner.

How to stay devoted?

Easy! Stay the hell-arious on your path of your choice, commitment, practice, and devotion by fiercely prioritizing your values of what beauty and beautiful means to you. Claim your birthright to live a beautiful life over and over—no matter the circumstances.

Sure, there will be plenty of less beautiful things, people, and moments in your adventure of life. It is supposed to be like that! Don't fuss over it too much, because quite frankly, nothing ever stays the same anyways. Instead, keep nurturing your devotion by using all non-bliss to fortify and clarify your momentum of who you really are. Re-choose, re-commit, re-practice, and re-grow your passion and devotion when things go differently than you want—turning even these moments into a nourishing and skillful shift to be something beautiful. Living that way means you have mastered changing what is judged as ugly, wrong, or troublesome in physical life to be what it really is—beauty.

Ask yourself: How does being devoted to living a beautiful life look and feel for you? What devotional practices are right for you? How do you sense yourself as being devoted and as a devoted being?

I left you plenty of pages to elaborate about your gorgeous devotion to beauty.

Important! Change it up with time—life is ever-changing, and so are you and your ways of nourishing your devotion. Today it's laying in the garden, and tomorrow it's jumping out of an airplane. How glorious is that?

To create a beautiful life, it takes your conscious choice and your serious commitment that is followed by your mindful practice; which creates your passion and nourishes your devotion.

Look around and focus on all beauty. Soon enough, you will believe and know that Life IS indeed beautiful!

_____

_____

_____

_____

_____

_____

_____

_____

_____

_____

_____

_____

_____

_____

_____

_____

_____

_____

_____

_____

STEP SIX: BE AND LIVE A BEAUTIFUL LIFE

What's all that pre-work going to be good for if you never harvest the fruition?

To BE, live, and show up in a confident readiness to expect a beautiful life is that harvested good you get to enjoy as soon as you allow yourself to receive and experience it.

What would keep you from allowing?

All your non-beautiful feelings and thoughts about yourself, others, happenings, and life itself.

Let this sink in for a minute!

This is important, because it makes the moment when you change to beautiful feelings and thoughts the split second when your allowing-it-all-in floodgates can open up—truly a happening that is worth celebrating!

How does that even look, to BE and live?

BE means that you as a whole being - body, mind, soul, and consciousness - are rightfully here, no mistake at all. Give yourself that right, you deserve it!

Live means that as your whole being - body, mind, soul, and consciousness - can experience life in all fullness. Give yourself that experience, you deserve it!

In truth, I picture you being ready to run around in your journey without giving a care to what others say, do, or want you to be.

Instead - in your craziest jump suit, colorful hair, or whatever you want it to be - you are dancing like you have never danced before. At least, not in this lifetime.

Alright, I might have gotten a little crazy here but you get the point! You are the only one that can have *your* party in your life—nobody can ever do it for you. I say, party!

This last step is to remind you that in order to successfully experience a beautiful life, you must also BE and live as such. You must act and behave as such!

The same goes for experiencing youthfulness, healthiness, love, success, abundance, or anything—as we covered in the chapter ***Nothing is Ever Set in Stone***.

This chapter also reminds you that you are in complete charge of how you live, and that with being and living a beautiful life right at this second, you are creating and manifesting your next new second—which will be a beautiful one too.

For this last step of the ***Six Steps to Live a Beautiful Life***, please ask yourself:

• How does "to BE and live a beautiful life" look and feel for you?

• What represents the art of living a beautiful life for you?

Close your eyes while remembering that you get to choose, commit, practice, grow a passion, and be devoted—then show up to BE and live as that mountain of bliss!

Write your absolute happiest and most beautiful ways, thoughts, and feelings down to create your own ecstatic tale—and keep adding and changing your story all the time, then see what happens for you!

To create a beautiful life, it takes your conscious choice and your serious commitment that is followed by your mindful practice; which creates your passion and nourishes your devotion to BE and live your beautiful life.

With such a great basis and hopefully a lot of eagerness to really experience your life as beautiful, I say, you are "riper than ripe" for the next step of claiming your own true story—to go dive into the adventure of your fake void.

What that's all about is explained in the next few chapters...

Look around and focus on all beauty. Soon enough, you will believe and know that Life IS indeed beautiful!

_____

_____

_____

_____

_____

_____

_____

_____

_____

_____

_____

_____

_____

_____

_____

_____

_____

_____

_____

_____

_____

_____

THE FAKE VOID

Fake is great! Just think of fake meat... There is no truth that it is meat, we get to decide to call it "fake-meat" or "plant-food," and we can either enjoy its meat-fake-ness or simply show no interest.

I love the energy of "fake" as it resembles that there is no truth-sticking to whatever it is that we call fake. We can make the fake whatever we want it to be—it is even possible to enjoy its fake-ness or leave it all together. Reminds me of how life works; we are in charge of what we call our truth or being fake, and what we enjoy or want to leave all together. There is so much room for freedom and creation in this!

The *fake void* is such a no truth-sticking entity, and you can bend it to what you want it to be—to enjoy its fake-ness or leave it all together.

Let me explain...

Have you ever gone backwards in your path of human life, beyond your physical starting point - your transformation into physicality - to where all you were was your energetic essence?

Have you ever re-felt this whole process of becoming you, not just from birth - which most of us have not done either - but from beyond being flesh and blood, when you were floating in consciousness as energy with everything and everyone, also energy, as one?

If not, you are in for a treat of re-remembering what your real true beauty, your real way of being beautiful, and the real beauty of your life is—what strength, knowing, and energetic-reasoning you had from the beginning, way before you showed up as your physical you.

You might wonder what crazy bug has taken over for me to write a book about a fake void, let alone what kind of reason there is behind the idea to take you way back in time.

The answer is easy. It was my own fake void that inspired me. Not remembering myself as a solely energetic essence or a human freshling until I was about 3 years old, left me feeling like I am missing out on knowing who I really am, and always was. I simply had no clue.

The dependency of other people filling that gap with *their* stories about me did not only feel unwell, it freaked me out, because I had this deep knowing that there is more about me, especially more truth. Questions and thoughts like, "How true is this story that others are telling about me?" and, "Shouldn't I tell my own story about myself?" took over my heart, which set my mind on fire, until my whole being was under siege. Dramatic, I know!

Stubborn and resourceful as I am - read more about my life journey in my book ***What it Means to BE a Woman*** - I could not let it be. I wanted to know who I am and who I always was. I wanted to tell my own story from *my* point of remembering, energetically and also physically. I called this "not remembering" my fake void—a gap in which others' stories about me have no truth-sticking. I knew that deep down I did know, and that through re-remembering, I can bend my tale into alignment with who I was, and who I am.

Since your story could look much different, more accurate, more you, and probably cooler too, wouldn't you want to know how widely separate they are—the story you were told and the story that is yours to tell? Because let's stay real here, what others are telling is not always accurate, and even if correct for them it is still not the story that you could tell.

Everyone creates their own reality, making *their* tale *their* reality, and no matter how much they love you, often your truth is left out of their story. For one, they don't know because only you know your truth. For two, their tale might simply be better for them. Or three, they have forgotten, since it was - and still is - too hurtful to hang on to how it really happened.

"But why even bother filling the old fake void, and not just focus on the *now* since that is all we have?" You might ask.

It is true that *now* is all you have, and is where change is possible. Finding and feeling yourself as a whole being in your *now* is crucial since, how you feel and think right now, creates your next new moment. However, if you can choose to build your *now* onto the foundation of the stories of others about you, or onto your truth - your own story - which one do you think is of deeper well-feeling and stronger self-connection?

Most people struggle with unfitting experiences from childhood. Heck, they go to therapy to talk about it, heal it, and to let go of it—all while re-telling, re-feeling, and re-creating the physical trauma anew and on a base of stories that others are telling.

In the meantime, a simple solution of re-remembering what that experience was from your energetic perspective - which is always true, never traumatic, and without exception always a calibration into your true being - is available. Just think what going to therapy from that point of being will achieve!

People lack their connection to their energetic essence and consciousness because they have been made to believe that all they are is physicality. Most don't know that they are a whole being made of a physical and energetic essence - body, mind, soul, and consciousness - let alone understand that a deep energetic intelligence, which is their clear knowing, is always available and present. So they go get help outside of them from sources that know nothing about their truth, all while basing the solutions they are seeking on tales that are not real—on the stories of others.

You say you can't remember. That is fake! Other people tell you your story. That is fake too, because it is *their* reality and not yours.

Filling your fake void with wisdom coming straight from your energetic essence, wipes out all negative and hurtful physical life programming that you are living—filing your fake void with your pure positive intelligence and true knowing. This inner work will be much more helpful than the hard work of trying to fix something that is grown on anything but your truth—and just to imagine that the problem might not even exist in your truth.

Energetically, you have all the answers. Energetically, you got this. That is what matters!

Digging deep and trying to figure out the *why* of all this is beyond the point, and would shift you into a frequency that is opposite of living a beautiful life—creating a lot of disturbances for you and everyone involved all while not giving you the slightest glimpse of your own story. The *why*, *what*, and *who* is simply not important, and just for giggles and an eye-roll, have you ever tried to convince anyone in your family that their way of remembering you is wrong?

I suggest to simply acquire the attitude of "It is what it is!" since this fake void-living has been going on for eons. Then, acknowledge that your fake void exists because you can work with something that you allow, and focus on re-remembering your energetic wisdom while filling your fake void without anyone else involved. Alone and in private!

Fact is that this fake void is an only in physical life entity because energetically, you always know, making it nonexisting in your soul essence. Through re-remembering as your soul being - where all information that you will ever need is stored and available for you - you can fill your fake void with your true story, sending it into nonexistence. How beautiful is that! Plus, to think that teaching this to children at an early age could avoid their fake void, is beyond exciting to me.

Fact is, also, that the fake void is grown and kept alive by living the old belief that you can't remember. Self-inflicted thoughts and actions, as listed below, are the culprit:

- I believe what is being said, even if it feels untrue

- I listen to the stories, even though I don't like hearing them

- I won't question the tales, even when I have so many questions

- I am not deciding if I like or don't like how others talk about me—I stay neutral because it's easier

- I am re-telling these tales, even when they seem off to me—hence, the stories about me don't feel good, even more they make me mad, or at its best I fight what is being said about me

It is about time you get off that huge gap of nonsense and fill your fake void with the wondrous flavor of your true and beautiful life essence—with the same enthusiasm as you would fill the fake void in an ice cream cone, with delicious ice cream that is.

Okay you got me—I love ice cream, hence the sweet treat remark. I have a great fake void filling story about buying so much ice cream, while in quarantine with my family, that nothing else fit in our freezer. Our grown kids thought that my husband and I went mad because we turned into ice cream-hoarders, when all we did was be amazed that they finally had ice cream at the store again. Definitely no more fake void in the freezer or the family laughter-department! I want your fake void to be like my freezer—filled with deliciousness that is yours to enjoy and tell.

Truth be told, I have travelled the path of re-discovering the feeling of beauty and beautiful all the way to ugliness and back, because hey, I am "only human" after all. Right?

Wrong! I realized that I was cutting myself short by being, showing up, acting as, feeling, thinking of myself, and experiencing life as "only human." The "only human" label comes with a clear limit of not being in control of how I experience my life or how I feel. It was keeping my fake void nourished with the stories of other people about me, and was aiding as a great excuse for not having to take responsibility for living my life the way I wanted, and want it, to be lived.

So an undeniable clarity set in:

It was time to re-focus, re-remember, and re-discover that I am in charge; that I have all the answers, at least energetically; that I can bring back my own story and reasons, in which living a beautiful life that is focused on beauty is all there is.

It was crystal clear that in order to get out of my funk of being "only human," I had to step into being my wholeness, which included filling my fake void with the purity of who I was, and who I am.

I want this for you too!

Through this fake void filing process you will be able to claim your complete remembrance of your own story through which you can look at the beautiful aspects of everything and everyone—no matter what is said or done right now or what was said or done back in time, and certainly without minding what others are brave enough to experience.

Are you ready to teleport back into re-being, re-feeling, re-remembering, and re-claiming what you really are and what the experience of physical life really is for you—what it was always meant to be for you? Are you curious and eager to dig in your energetic goldmine and fill your fake void?

If so, hold on tight, you are in for an adventurous ride...

Look around and focus on all beauty. Soon enough, you will believe and know that Life IS indeed beautiful!

FILLING THE FAKE VOID

You have the power to awaken beauty and infuse what was - your childhood and beyond - and what is - your now and furthermore - with that beauty!

The famous saying, "I don't remember the time when I was little, let alone before being a human," is false, bears no truth, and creates an energy of being powerless. Of course you remember!

If you use that phrase to get out of something - like, "I don't remember how fast I drove" - it might actually create a pocket of power in the sense of how not-knowing at the right moment can be of help in physical life—but that is not the remembering that I am writing about here.

Energetically and soulfully you always remember and always know who you where, who you are, and who you will be, because consciousness is where all intelligence is stored. Only when you show up separate and disconnected from your energetic essence, solely as your physical you, will you not remember. Makes sense, since physicality is limited.

This brings clarity to what essence - your physical or your energetic - you are experiencing your life through:

• When the scenario of not remembering is present, you are only physical

• When you have clear access to all the remembering, you are energetic

Tapping into your energetic knowing while using your mind and feelings, then basing your physical life actions on that wisdom, means that you are aligned as your whole being; body, mind, soul, and consciousness—a very powerful way to BE and live!

So if you catch yourself not remembering, stop right in your tracks by recalling that you are in your self-limiting path and stuck-ness by experiencing only as your physical essence - the most non-remembering place for you to look for real answers, at least most of the times - whereas in your energetic essence, in which you are not pinching off your remembering, you will always recall and clearly know. Yes, this asks for your unconditional trust in your inner voice, often felt like a knowing without any trace of where it is coming from; a bit mystical and magical, but life in itself is mystical and magical, so why not trust that hunch a little more and then even a little more.

In the following chapters I will take you on your journey to re-remember it all—or at least as much as you are allowing yourself to re-know again.

Important! These exercises and practices have nothing to do with knowing exactly how everything in your life will unfold in your future. Where would the surprising fun be in that? Instead, they will help you fill your "I don't remember" gap, because besides being not real it is usually filled with lots of untruth or shall we say "gunk!"

Having your fake void filled with your truth brings on a powerful centered-ness and grounded-ness that carries you deeply and strongly though your life, and what's ahead of you.

Just think how mighty it is to:

• Know the _essence_ you were from the beginning and beyond

• Understand the _energetic_ and _physical_ value you chose, arriving as a human being

• Remember the _reasons_ for choosing to be alive

• Feel your _truth_ of your becoming

• Recall the momentum and your _energy_ of your arrival on earth

- Recollect the *essence* of yourself in your years of not remembering

You will be able to re-remember what you were and are all about—from your perspective, your knowing, your understanding and your point of truth. If embraced, this is a practice of re-birth and becoming whole. Some even say that old engraved pain and sadness that they never could get to, is being stirred up because of working through this method, making it possible to cleanse it out for good. If so, embrace this happening by acknowledging your feelings and welcoming the clarity they bring for you—a clarity in the sense of realizing that most of these rock-hard and old unwell-feelings are not even yours, but someone else's, who told you a story from their point of beliefs. Consciously accepting this lets you separate what is yours from what is not yours—creating the opportune chance to let go of all that is grown on foreign land by simply just letting it disappear into nothingness.

Celebrate that cleansing with gratitude and a full heart!

What's left is your gold to work with. Yes, your feelings are worth gold and working with them is your golden opportunity for self-growth. The beauty of it all is that, by working through the next few chapters, you will re-write, re-shape, and re-mold that gold into something that you will feel good about, that you will love, and that you will be exited to tell. It is your own truthful and golden story! Through gaining your historic truth you can then make confident choices and decisions that are based on your unquestioned knowing - not on the opinions of others about you - of who you are. Your golden version of YOU!

And just to thought-check...

If you think that this traveling back will be hard or even impossible for you, it is not! You are an already trained traveling back-er. Just think how many times you take the effort to travel into your past by talking about - and re-feeling - something beautiful, hurtful, or incredibly hard that has happened to you, or even better, that someone else experienced. You know exactly how to travel back, everyone does! We were conditioned from early age on and witnessed others practicing this without end. The only difference is that now, I am guiding you to find your magical essence for the sake of becoming whole in your being and life, through re-remembering how beautifully it all started for you.

Filling your fake void is like filling your treasure trunk—with riches that you want to cherish!

Are you ready?

Fair warning; as also mentioned in the chapter *A Star IS Living*—the next few chapters are similarly written. That is on purpose to keep this process simple, easy to follow, and like a journal. Plus, if you ever re-read your entries, since it is intentionally in a flowing style, it will feel like you are reading a book about you and how it all started.

Look around and focus on all beauty. Soon enough, you will believe and know that Life IS indeed beautiful!

A STAR IS IN BETWEEN ALL STARS

And so it always was...

Once upon a time, way before you came into being flesh and blood, there was this energetic essence made of pure positive energy floating somewhere out in the infinite—being one with all, having no worries in the world, and with only one grand wish in mind:

To enter physical life as your human you.

Already, you understood that your longing for this process of becoming, the creation of your physical body, the adventure of living, and the feeling of yourself as human is beautiful—and was needed by you and one-ness to expand and calibrate into more. You knew that real beauty was and is awaiting you in this physical world; in all its variable forms, ways, and means.

I bet that it never even crossed your mind to go all the way back, let alone think about having the ability to go experience this only-energetic-before-human part of you. But here you are, and you can! Energetically, you know exactly what value this phase has for you, what it means to you, how it feels for you, and that it indeed is the biggest and most intelligent part of you.

You know that you are pure, fresh, and beautiful as your energy, and that questioning this travel experience is impossible—leaving you no other choice than to go. So go! Travel to this beautiful energetic place where butterflies are in your tummy, warmness is in your heart, and electric jolts are running through your whole being—all while feeling one with consciousness.

Find a wonderful space for you to close your eyes. Breathe fully and deeply into this sacred travel beyond your physical time—where all you are is your precious energetic essence with a deep longing to become a human being. Allow yourself to get lost in the bliss of feeling yourself into this energetic stage:

- Sense how being your energy feels for you. Do you feel light, fresh, clear, and at ease?

- Sense your intentions before you transitioned into physical. Is your plan to be relaxed, free, knowing, and peaceful as your human being?

- Sense the promises you made to yourself once being alive. Did you tell yourself that you will feel enjoyment, fulfillment, happiness, and bliss?

- Sense your deepest knowing. Is it clear to you that you are deserving, loving, and supposed to BE?

What *energetic* wisdom are you getting?

Take the first impressions you receive; be it words, visions, feelings, or sensations. Don't worry if they don't make complete sense right away, instead, trust your heart and feel into the well-feeling of this guidance. This profound knowing - with an origin that you can't always pinpoint - is coming from your deepest inner truth, your soul, your intuition, your most accurate intelligence. It is always correct, on point, and has your best interest at heart. It was your truth back then, it is your truth now, and it always will be your truth!

Trust by really laying into feeling all this wisdom. Welcome it freely! Fill every single cell of yourself to the brim with the beauty of re-awakening, re-remembering, re-feeling, and re-writing your truthful story on your cellular level.

Next, write about it! Journaling imbeds the information as a deeper imprint or shift—your sensing is energy, your thoughts and feelings are energy, and your written words are energy. This means triple the magic and - in this case - the more the better, which also means the sturdier. Plus, if you ever have the facepalm moment of being unsure or are forgetful all around, you can always flip through your words with the confidence that whatever is written is real—because you sensed it and wrote it while being in alignment with who you really are.

The next few pages are reserved for you to write about your travel-back-in-time experience. Don't hold back, put it all into words, for you to never forget what incredible essence you are made of. Keep in mind that future add-ons and changes are completely legit.

Make this the entry of your life, because it is!

Then, go and show up as your newly supercharged you, act like it, and use your mind to choose deliberately all that is aligned with this wonderful energetic version of you. BE and live this shift that you have accomplished.

Important! These feelings are unique for everyone—it is supposed to be like that. That's why I am not going to say what they have to be, or the outcome that this journal entry must have. It might also take a few times until you really get the sense for this type of work, since it might not be the norm of what you have been practicing or been taught to do. This is not a one-time exercise—rather, it is meant to be performed many times, over and over as a journey, if you will. Some sensing might be of bliss right at the first try, while for others it might spark sadness, fear, anger, or old unwell-feelings at first. This is normal. It is also not unusual if today, it's pure bliss, and next time it's a sense of anything but bliss. That is okay too! Remember, you are cleansing out any untruth - fear, anger, sadness - to get to your core of your pure positive energy. Think of it like layers—your first time sensing, a layer of sadness might show itself; next time you sense, a layer of anger; next time, it is all bliss and you are at your core of being pure positive energy. Once that happens, experiencing this beautiful part of you will give you a sense of what you are feeling for, moving forward in your life—it's like a north star for you to focus on.

Keep an open mind and continue with your sensing in lighthearted-ness, awe, and joyful-ness. Whenever it will resonate, and whatever this brings forth for you, it is perfect, for you!

Your new beginning - your new story - will be written little by little every time you come back to this. Make it on *your* terms and base it on *when* and *how* it is best for you!

Look around and focus on all beauty. Soon enough, you will believe and know that Life IS indeed beautiful!

_____

_____

_____

_____

_____

_____

_____

_____

_____

_____

_____

_____

_____

_____

_____

_____

_____

_____

_____

_____

_____

A STAR IS IN THE MAKING

Your plan is created...

Wishing, wanting, and desiring to enter this physical world so strongly and determinedly and with no room for denial, what did your energetic essence do?

The only logical thing!

Find the perfect team of a host and a co-creator; your Mom and Dad! Then, everyone in perfect place and without any delay, you all went into action to create your physical you in your personal human host - your Mom or carrier - for you to grow, and eventually, dance around alive as your unique and beautiful human being.

Joy and excitement entered the equation! Your own delight as your energetic essence, that was about to join your humanness was literally limitless. You couldn't wait! Your already physically existent parent's glee to experience the adventure of their own little one becoming a baby and join their lives very soon, was literally exploding. They couldn't wait either! Just think of all that firework energy!

In the possibility of this creation phase being anything but heavenly, peaceful, or loving - involving rape, force, drugs or such - it is very valuable to re-write the start of your human story. Re-remembering and re-feeling what this phase was for *you* through *your* energetic essence while leaving everything else out means that you replace their history with your truth. If that makes you wonder if denial is part of this step, not at all! The only denial that was present in all those years was denying your truth by living other people's stories about you, and your making.

This work here is for *you* to fill *your* fake void with *your* true essence—the details are in your energy and consciousness, ready for you to re-remember and re-feel.

That's your cue to please find a beautiful space and some precious time to close your eyes, breathe, and relax into this graceful phase of your life. Imagine traveling back in time so you can feel what this "in the process of your creation" essence is for you in real time.

How do you sense yourself as energy in your commitment to be in physical life?

Are you excited, determined, and knowingly sure? Can you feel that, no matter through what energy you are created, it is your perfect experience? Are you creative, playful, and feeling like you can't wait? Are you open to physical life? Are you choosing to take responsibility for all that is you? What intentions, expectations, and promises do you have?

What *energetic* wisdom are you getting?

Feel, hear, see, taste, smell, and think of what you are re-remembering, re-feeling, and re-knowing about this time—leave the opinions of others out of this experience.

Listen with laser-sharp focus and don't even think about brushing any of that wisdom away as nonsense, or even worse, be in disbelief or count it as untrue. It is all true! It is all you!

What are you waiting for? Go write it all down! I left you some pages…

Then show up as your newly supercharged you, act like it, and use your mind to choose deliberately all that is aligned with this wonderful new version of you. BE and live this shift that you have accomplished.

Don't forget:

Important! These feelings are unique for everyone—it is supposed to be like that. That's why I am not going to say what they have to be, or the outcome that this journal entry must have. It might also take a few times until you really get the sense for this type of work, since it might not be the norm of what you have been practicing or been taught to do. This is not a one-time exercise—rather, it is meant to be performed many times, over and over as a journey, if you will. Some sensing might be of bliss right at the first try, while for others it might spark sadness, fear, anger, or old unwell-feelings at first. This is normal. It is also not unusual if today, it's pure bliss, and next time it's a sense of anything but bliss. That is okay too! Remember, you are cleansing out any untruth - fear, anger, sadness - to get to your core of your pure positive energy. Think of it like layers—your first time sensing, a layer of sadness might show itself; next time you sense, a layer of anger; next time, it is all bliss and you are at your core of being pure positive energy. Once that happens, experiencing this beautiful part of you will give you a sense of what you are feeling for, moving forward in your life—it's like a north star for you to focus on.

Keep an open mind and continue with your sensing in lighthearted-ness, awe, and joyful-ness. Whenever it will resonate, and whatever this brings forth for you, it is perfect, for you!

Your new beginning - your new story - will be written little by little every time you come back to this. Make it on *your* terms and base it on *when* and *how* it is best for you!

Look around and focus on all beauty. Soon enough, you will believe and know that Life IS indeed beautiful!

_____

_____

_____

_____

_____

_____

_____

_____

_____

_____

_____

_____

_____

_____

_____

_____

_____

_____

_____

A STAR IS CREATED

And so it begins...

Next comes the physical fact we all know—you are growing, growing, and growing in your dear momma's physical body to the exploding point where you are outgrowing her palace and her hostess abilities. Her womb represents a place of light, preparing you for the beauty that is awaiting you outside her protection and nourishment. A precious time indeed!

In physical life, the stories about you that your Mom, Dad, and others are telling make sense and seem to complete your life story. But is that really the case? Where is your energetic essence in this, besides being the main physical character that everyone talks about?

Again: In the possibility of this creation phase being anything but heavenly, peacefully, or loving it is very valuable to re-write this part of your human story. Re-remembering and re-feeling what this phase was for *you* through *your* energetic essence while leaving everything else out means that you replace their history with your truth. If that makes you wonder if denial is part of this step, not at all! The only denial that was present in all those years was denying your truth by living other people's stories about you and your creation.

This is your invitation to re-feel yourself into your essence of your growing-time, into the embracing nature and comfort in the womb, into the gratefulness that programmed your cells because you were feeling home and safe in this time of your life. Be open and let this wisdom surface, believe that you always had that information - energetically, at least - and embrace the truth of it all.

Close your eyes and observe the safety in the womb - of being given everything you needed, no matter the circumstances or intentions of your mom - for you to energetically BE and physically BEcome.

What are you sensing? How is the womb feeling for you? Who are you in your mom's palace? What are you feeling as you? What are your wishes and expectations for your life? How is your heart feeling—is it full of love?

What *energetic* wisdom are you getting?

Feel, hear, see, taste, smell, and think of what you are re-remembering, re-feeling, and re-knowing about this time—leave the opinions of others out of this experience.

Listen with laser-sharp focus, and don't even think about brushing any of that wisdom away as nonsense—or even worse, be in disbelief or count it as untrue. It is all true! It is all you!

When ready, over the next few pages, write your exact words that are flowing from your gracious heart. This fills every single cell of your whole being and shifts you to a frequency of safety, besides complete-ness.

Then, go and show up as your newly supercharged you. Act like it—use your mind to choose deliberately all that is aligned with this wonderful energetic version of you. BE and live this shift that you have accomplished.

Keep in mind:

Important! These feelings are unique for everyone—it is supposed to be like that. That's why I am not going to say what they have to be, or the outcome that this journal entry must have. It might also take a few times until you really get the sense for this type of work, since it might not be the norm of what you have been practicing or been taught to do. This is not a one-time exercise—rather, it is meant to be performed many times, over and over as a journey, if you will. Some sensing might be of bliss right at the first try, while for others it might spark sadness, fear, anger, or old unwell-feelings at first. This is normal. It is also not unusual if today, it's pure bliss, and next time it's a sense of anything but bliss. That is okay too! Remember, you are cleansing out any untruth - fear, anger, sadness - to get to your core of your pure positive energy. Think of it like layers—your first time sensing, a layer of sadness might show itself; next time you sense, a layer of anger; next time, it is all bliss and you are at your core of being pure positive energy. Once that happens, experiencing this beautiful part of you will give you a sense of what you are feeling for, moving forward in your life—it's like a north star for you to focus on.

Keep an open mind and continue with your sensing in lighthearted-ness, awe, and joyful-ness. Whenever it will resonate, and whatever this brings forth for you, it is perfect, for you!

Your new beginning - your new story - will be written little by little every time you come back to this. Make it on *your* terms and base it on *when* and *how* it is best for you!

Look around and focus on all beauty. Soon enough, you will believe and know that Life IS indeed beautiful!

_____

_____

_____

_____

_____

_____

_____

_____

_____

_____

_____

_____

_____

_____

_____

_____

_____

_____

A STAR IS BORN

Physicality just hit...

You were indeed very well prepared for all beauty - and to see, hear, taste, smell, think, and feel the beauty - in everything and everyone when you took your first breath as your physical human you.

That first breath is what you want to focus on in this chapter.

Feel and breathe into this glorious moment!

You might say, "I don't remember that moment." What a human thing to believe! That's your fake void speaking—filled by stories of other people and fed by re-living your old beliefs and habits. As your energetic essence, the sense of your first breath is always available for you to re-remember. If you let it, it will be as clear as water, filling every single cell of your whole being with an awakening healing-sensation that will feed straight into your heart.

That first breath is what started your physical adventure on Mother Earth. It goes without further explanation why it is worth a gemstone to recall and re-celebrate it as the grown you that you are now, since you probably have not done that with the grand graciousness it deserves.

We celebrate birthdays every year, but that is not the same celebration like the one of your first breath. It is the celebration of how long you have lived. Your first breath represents the momentum of your willingness to live, the power of pushing through, and the beginning of the oxygenation that will carry you until you transition back to 100% energy again. It's a lifelong breath-ship, if you will!

Time to celebrate!

Close your eyes and get your nowadays-bottom to your incredible first breath. Sink deeply into the truth of this first breath of life.

What *energetic* wisdom are you getting?

Re-remember your hopes, clarity, and intentions. Re-feel your love, excitement, and freshness. Re-think the plans for yourself! Re-taste the air, re-sniff the smells, re-see the moment, re-hear the sounds. Re-know the preciousness that your start of your new life is, while leaving the opinions of others out of this experience.

Listen with laser-sharp focus and don't even think about brushing any of that wisdom away as nonsense—or even worse, be in disbelief or count it as untrue. I promise that - even if on the physical life level another story is being told - energetically, your arrival means the world to you. So fill every single cell of yours with this celebratory energy; even better, light a candle and re-celebrate it all over again as a testament to your truth of being you.

Then write passionately about your birth, your arrival, your coming into physicality, and your first breath. Leave nothing out and make it the most beautiful story that you have ever heard, ever witnessed, and have ever seen—because it is!

Furthermore, go and show up as your newly supercharged you, act like it, and use your mind to choose deliberately all that is aligned with this wonderful energetic version of you. BE and live this shift that you have accomplished.

And once again:

Important! These feelings are unique for everyone—it is supposed to be like that. That's why I am not going to say what they have to be, or the outcome that this journal entry must have. It might also take a few times until you really get the sense for this type of work, since it might not be the norm of what you have been practicing or been taught to do. This is not a one-time exercise—rather, it is meant to be performed many times, over and over as a journey, if you will. Some sensing might be of bliss right at the first try, while for others it might spark sadness, fear, anger, or old unwell-feelings at first. This is normal. It is also not unusual if today, it's pure bliss, and next time it's a sense of anything but bliss. That is okay too! Remember, you are cleansing out any untruth - fear, anger, sadness - to get to your core of your pure positive energy. Think of it like layers—your first time sensing, a layer of sadness might show itself; next time you sense, a layer of anger; next time, it is all bliss and you are at your core of being pure positive energy. Once that happens, experiencing this beautiful part of you will give you a sense of what you are feeling for, moving forward in your life—it's like a north star for you to focus on.

Keep an open mind and continue with your sensing in lighthearted-ness, awe, and joyful-ness. Whenever it will resonate, and whatever this brings forth for you, it is perfect, for you!

Your new beginning - your new story - will be written little by little every time you come back to this. Make it on *your* terms and base it on *when* and *how* it is best for you!

Look around and focus on all beauty. Soon enough, you will believe and know that Life IS indeed beautiful!

_____

_____

_____

_____

_____

_____

_____

_____

_____

_____

_____

_____

_____

_____

_____

_____

_____

_____

_____

A STAR IS LIVING

Wildly in love with living physical life, to the point where others are convinced that you are crazy...

So here you are, in the midst of all beauty and as your whole beautiful human being that includes:

- Your energetic essence that is always the root of you—your biggest and most intelligent part that transitions with you - and as you - from purely energy, to physicality, back to purely energy

- Your physical body, your host to make this wild ride of a life possible - a masterpiece living the energetically guided masterplan - by serving the physical journey that is put in motion by your energetic essence

- Your heart that hosts and serves your energetic essence and its information—guiding and manifesting through feelings

- Your mind, which serves your heart and its information, to complete the manifestations through the capability of focusing your thoughts

- Your consciousness; serving as your connection to be one with all—it has unlimited information and gives you the essence of confidence to BE

Most of your later life you don't have to re-remember, re-feel, re-see, or re-know, because you are in it right now. But often, life-business takes over by pulling you into being only in your physicality. Combine that with living the falseness of other people's tales about your little you, and disalignment takes over. This results in feelings like fear, helplessness, not knowing, exhaustion, and an allover unwell-feeling—creating a life that is hard to live. That's when creating a balance between your physical existence and energetic being is helpful. Sometimes, being lopsided on purpose and only being energetic for a while, is even better.

Questions like the ones below - and re-reading the chapter *Nothing is Ever Set in Stone* - can help you re-gain balance:

• Are you consciously aware of your feelings, desires, and the wisdom that is clearly being offered to you by your soul being and your heart?

• Are you constantly aligning yourself with your energetic essence in order to experience your soul passion and live your soul journey?

With that said and asked…

Let's re-focus and get back to filling what really needs to be filled; your early years of physicality that you say you don't remember!

Take your pen, and don't be shy to remember even the parts about you that seem unbelievable. What you heard so far is how others experienced you, saw you, and recall events of your early presence. Those tales have nothing to do with how it really was for *you*, let alone what *you* are really made of.

Here is my fair warning again—the next few chapters are similarly written. That is on purpose to keep this process simple, easy to follow, and like a journal. Plus, if you ever re-read your entries, since it is intentionally in a flowing style, it will feel like you are reading a book about your early years.

Look around and focus on all beauty. Soon enough, you will believe and know that Life IS indeed beautiful!

ZERO-TO-ONE YEAR OLD

Get all comfy, close your eyes, and keep them closed until it's time for you to scribble about your experience.

Imagine entering a time capsule - or something of that kind - to travel backwards in your existence. Breathe into feeling yourself being your little zero-to-one year old star. Keep in mind to do that with excitement, and give yourself a smile.

You ARE NOW zero-to-one!

What happens in that time for *you*? What is your truth of essence as that age? How do you feel, what do you think; what energetic information is there for you? Are you pumped to be here? Are you a superhero, a leader, a creative dreamer, or observer? What are your promises to yourself? What are your desires and wishes for yourself? Who are you right then and now, as a zero-to-one year old you?

Being a whole year in this time of physicality, what *energetic* wisdom are you getting?

Stay in your perspective and your feelings—leave the viewpoints of others on physical life out of this. Certainly don't buy into what others said or say about you; instead, only feel and sense what your energetic and physical truth was back then - correction, since you took a time capsule - are right now.

Believe into the first sensing that comes in for you; be it feelings, visions, imaginations, words, or other hints—they are true because you are the one receiving them.

Stay in this wonderful adventure as long as you like. When ready, open your eyes and start writing all that goodness down. This is your true energetic and physical essence of being your zero-to-one year old! The next few pages are all yours.

Just to clarify again:

Important! These feelings are unique for everyone—it is supposed to be like that. That's why I am not going to say what they have to be, or the outcome that this journal entry must have. It might also take a few times until you really get the sense for this type of work, since it might not be the norm of what you have been practicing or been taught to do. This is not a one-time exercise—rather, it is meant to be performed many times, over and over as a journey, if you will. Some sensing might be of bliss right at the first try, while for others it might spark sadness, fear, anger, or old unwell-feelings at first. This is normal. It is also not unusual if today, it's pure bliss, and next time it's a sense of anything but bliss. That is okay too! Remember, you are cleansing out any untruth - fear, anger, sadness - to get to your core of your pure positive energy. Think of it like layers—your first time sensing, a layer of sadness might show itself; next time you sense, a layer of anger; next time, it is all bliss and you are at your core of being pure positive energy. Once that happens, experiencing this beautiful part of you will give you a sense of what you are feeling for, moving forward in your life—it's like a north star for you to focus on.

Keep an open mind and continue with your sensing in lighthearted-ness, awe, and joyful-ness. Whenever it will resonate, and whatever this brings forth for you, it is perfect, for you!

Your new beginning - your new story - will be written little by little every time you come back to this. Make it on *your* terms and base it on *when* and *how* it is best for you!

Look around and focus on all beauty. Soon enough, you will believe and know that Life IS indeed beautiful!

ONE-TO-TWO YEARS OLD

Continue to build onto the clarity you gained of being your zero-to-one year old—but now with the focus on being your little one-to-two years old you.

Get all comfy, close your eyes, and keep them closed until it's time for you to scribble about your experience.

Imagine entering a time capsule - or something of that kind - to travel backwards in your existence. Breathe into feeling yourself being your little one-to-two year old star. Keep in mind to do that with excitement, and give yourself a smile.

You ARE NOW one-to-two years old!

What is it like being you? What is your intuition telling you? Are you a mover and shaker energy, a busy body, or are you ever slowing down as you; are you loud or quiet? Who are you right now?

Being a whole year in this time of physicality, what *energetic* wisdom are you getting?

No matter what everyone else tells you about who and how you were at that age, remember that is only true for them in *their* physical life experience. Give yourself permission to go energetic, where you always know who you really are. It is *are,* not were, because ***hello***, you took a time capsule.

Believe into the first sensing that comes in for you; be it feelings, visions, imaginations, words, or other hints—they are true because you are the one receiving them!

Stay in this wonderful adventure as long as you like. When ready, open your eyes and start writing all that goodness down. This is your true energetic and physical essence of being one-to-two years old! The next few pages are all yours.

A friendly reminder:

Important! These feelings are unique for everyone—it is supposed to be like that. That's why I am not going to say what they have to be, or the outcome that this journal entry must have. It might also take a few times until you really get the sense for this type of work, since it might not be the norm of what you have been practicing or been taught to do. This is not a one-time exercise—rather, it is meant to be performed many times, over and over as a journey, if you will. Some sensing might be of bliss right at the first try, while for others it might spark sadness, fear, anger, or old unwell-feelings at first. This is normal. It is also not unusual if today, it's pure bliss, and next time it's a sense of anything but bliss. That is okay too! Remember, you are cleansing out any untruth - fear, anger, sadness - to get to your core of your pure positive energy. Think of it like layers—your first time sensing, a layer of sadness might show itself; next time you sense, a layer of anger; next time, it is all bliss and you are at your core of being pure positive energy. Once that happens, experiencing this beautiful part of you will give you a sense of what you are feeling for, moving forward in your life—it's like a north star for you to focus on.

Keep an open mind and continue with your sensing in lighthearted-ness, awe, and joyful-ness. Whenever it will resonate, and whatever this brings forth for you, it is perfect, for you!

Your new beginning - your new story - will be written little by little every time you come back to this. Make it on *your* terms and base it on *when* and *how* it is best for you!

Look around and focus on all beauty. Soon enough, you will believe and know that Life IS indeed beautiful!

_____

_____

_____

_____

_____

_____

_____

_____

_____

_____

_____

_____

_____

_____

_____

_____

_____

_____

_____

_____

_____

_____

_____

_____

_____

_____

_____

_____

_____

_____

_____

_____

_____

_____

_____

_____

_____

_____

_____

_____

_____

_____

TWO-TO-THREE YEARS OLD

Keep going, your story is just getting started! Grow on top of the truth that you already have gained by re-remembering yourself being zero-to-two years old—now, focus on being two-to-three years old.

Get all comfy, close your eyes, and keep them closed until it's time for you to scribble about your experience.

Imagine entering a time capsule - or something of that kind - to travel backwards in your existence. Breathe into feeling yourself being your little two-to-three year old star. Keep in mind to do that with excitement, and give yourself a smile.

You ARE NOW two-to-three years old!

What is it like being two-to-three years old? Who are you right now? What are you sensing—what is coming in for you? Are you a power being, a playful goof ball, a creative producing machine? Are you a silly in-the-moment energy, or as still and observing as can be? What are your thoughts? What promises are you making to yourself? What essence are you made of?

Being a whole year in this time of physicality, what *energetic* wisdom are you getting?

Go with your gut feeling, your intuition, your inner voice, and with what your heart is telling you. Take only *that* wisdom as your truth—no added artificial flavors of how it was for others is needed here. You and your re-remembering are enough!

Believe into the first sensing that comes in for you; be it feelings, visions, imaginations, words, or other hints—they are true because you are the one receiving them!

Stay in this wonderful adventure as long as you like. When ready, open your eyes and start writing all that goodness down.

This is your true energetic and physical essence of being two-to-three years old! The next few pages are all yours.

Here is my wonderful memo again:

Important! These feelings are unique for everyone—it is supposed to be like that. That's why I am not going to say what they have to be, or the outcome that this journal entry must have. It might also take a few times until you really get the sense for this type of work, since it might not be the norm of what you have been practicing or been taught to do. This is not a one-time exercise—rather, it is meant to be performed many times, over and over as a journey, if you will. Some sensing might be of bliss right at the first try, while for others it might spark sadness, fear, anger, or old unwell-feelings at first. This is normal. It is also not unusual if today, it's pure bliss, and next time it's a sense of anything but bliss. That is okay too! Remember, you are cleansing out any untruth - fear, anger, sadness - to get to your core of your pure positive energy. Think of it like layers—your first time sensing, a layer of sadness might show itself; next time you sense, a layer of anger; next time, it is all bliss and you are at your core of being pure positive energy. Once that happens, experiencing this beautiful part of you will give you a sense of what you are feeling for, moving forward in your life—it's like a north star for you to focus on.

Keep an open mind and continue with your sensing in lighthearted-ness, awe, and joyful-ness. Whenever it will resonate, and whatever this brings forth for you, it is perfect, for you!

Your new beginning - your new story - will be written little by little every time you come back to this. Make it on *your* terms and base it on *when* and *how* it is best for you!

Look around and focus on all beauty. Soon enough, you will believe and know that Life IS indeed beautiful!

_____

_____

_____

_____

_____

_____

_____

_____

_____

_____

_____

_____

_____

_____

_____

_____

_____

_____

_____

_____

_____

THREE-TO-FOUR YEARS OLD

Go on to build atop the foundation of you re-remembering yourself being zero-to-three years old. You are more complete than ever at this point—just think how much more you grow by focusing on being three-to-four years old.

Get all comfy, close your eyes, and keep them closed until it's time for you to scribble about your experience.

Imagine entering a time capsule - or something of that kind - to travel backwards in your existence. Breathe into feeling yourself being your little three-to-four year old star. Keep in mind to do that with excitement, and give yourself a smile.

You ARE NOW three-to-four years old!

What is this time for you? Who are you now? Are you a fighter, or a relaxer? What are your dreams about? How do you see your perfectly chosen future for you? What essence are you made of?

Being a whole year in this time of physicality, what *energetic* wisdom are you getting?

Believe in what is coming up for you—into the first sensing that comes in for you; be it feelings, visions, imaginations, words, or other hints, they are true, because you are the one receiving them! It is your real story of who you are, without any tales or experiences of other people.

Stay in this wonderful adventure as long as you like. When ready, open your eyes and start writing all that goodness down. This is your true energetic and physical essence of being three-to-four years old! The next few pages are all yours.

Remember:

Important! These feelings are unique for everyone—it is supposed to be like that. That's why I am not going to say what they have to be, or the outcome that this journal entry must have. It might also take a few times until you really get the sense for this type of work, since it might not be the norm of what you have been practicing or been taught to do. This is not a one-time exercise—rather, it is meant to be performed many times, over and over as a journey, if you will. Some sensing might be of bliss right at the first try, while for others it might spark sadness, fear, anger, or old unwell-feelings at first. This is normal. It is also not unusual if today, it's pure bliss, and next time it's a sense of anything but bliss. That is okay too! Remember, you are cleansing out any untruth - fear, anger, sadness - to get to your core of your pure positive energy. Think of it like layers—your first time sensing, a layer of sadness might show itself; next time you sense, a layer of anger; next time, it is all bliss and you are at your core of being pure positive energy. Once that happens, experiencing this beautiful part of you will give you a sense of what you are feeling for, moving forward in your life—it's like a north star for you to focus on.

Keep an open mind and continue with your sensing in lighthearted-ness, awe, and joyful-ness. Whenever it will resonate, and whatever this brings forth for you, it is perfect, for you!

Your new beginning - your new story - will be written little by little every time you come back to this. Make it on *your* terms and base it on *when* and *how* it is best for you!

Look around and focus on all beauty. Soon enough, you will believe and know that Life IS indeed beautiful!

_____

_____

_____

_____

_____

_____

_____

_____

_____

_____

_____

_____

_____

_____

_____

_____

_____

_____

_____

FOUR-TO-FIVE YEARS OLD

Let's do one more year, in case you still don't remember!

Build the pyramid of your truth by stacking onto the last few years of wisdom you gained—now with a determined focus on being four-to-five years old!

Get all comfy, close your eyes, and keep them closed until it's time for you to scribble about your experience.

Imagine entering a time capsule - or something of that kind - to travel backwards in your existence. Breathe into feeling yourself being your little four-to-five year old star. Keep in mind to do that with excitement, and give yourself a smile.

You ARE NOW four-to-five years old!

Who are you now? What are your hopes, happiness, and giggles made of? Are you feeling invincible? Are you feeling strong? Are you unstoppable?

Being a whole year in this time of physicality, what *energetic* wisdom are you getting?

Make sure not to mix any information that you heard from your outside field with your sensing—this work is only for *you*, and about *you*! Sensing your energetic part of you is a very private and unique practice. Enjoy it as that!

Believe in what is coming up for you—into the first sensing that comes in for you; be it feelings, visions, imaginations, words, or other hints, they are true, because you are the one receiving them! It is your real story of who you are.

Stay in this wonderful adventure as long as you like. When ready, open your eyes and start writing all that goodness down. This is your true energetic and physical essence of being four-to-five years old! The next few pages are all yours.

To recap:

Important! These feelings are unique for everyone—it is supposed to be like that. That's why I am not going to say what they have to be, or the outcome that this journal entry must have. It might also take a few times until you really get the sense for this type of work, since it might not be the norm of what you have been practicing or been taught to do. This is not a one-time exercise—rather, it is meant to be performed many times, over and over as a journey, if you will. Some sensing might be of bliss right at the first try, while for others it might spark sadness, fear, anger, or old unwell-feelings at first. This is normal. It is also not unusual if today, it's pure bliss, and next time it's a sense of anything but bliss. That is okay too! Remember, you are cleansing out any untruth - fear, anger, sadness - to get to your core of your pure positive energy. Think of it like layers—your first time sensing, a layer of sadness might show itself; next time you sense, a layer of anger; next time, it is all bliss and you are at your core of being pure positive energy. Once that happens, experiencing this beautiful part of you will give you a sense of what you are feeling for, moving forward in your life—it's like a north star for you to focus on.

Keep an open mind and continue with your sensing in lighthearted-ness, awe, and joyful-ness. Whenever it will resonate, and whatever this brings forth for you, it is perfect, for you!

Your new beginning - your new story - will be written little by little every time you come back to this. Make it on *your* terms and base it on *when* and *how* it is best for you!

Look around and focus on all beauty. Soon enough, you will believe and know that Life IS indeed beautiful!

FURTHERMORE...

If desired, you can keep going with this practice until your present age. For some, the essence of who they are is diluted with everyone else's and the world's opinions—even as adults. This practice is a nice way to clean it all up - privately and without anyone else involved - to then step into one-ness with yourself and claim your birthright of re-remembering, re-believing, re-knowing, and re-understanding your truth.

Year by year, you can re-remember and re-know the essence of who you are and your real story—like rolling up your red carpet from then to now, for you to walk your life journey on.

As mentioned before, in cases of abuse, brutality, drugs, or experiences of that type, this work is very helpful—fill yourself with the essence of your own truth by re-remembering what *you* are all about. It's a truly eye-opening, healing, cleansing, and empowering practice that will support you now and in your life to come.

It is never too late for this type of healing process!

These exercises are great for children too. Ask them to fill *their* own story—to re-remember who they are from an early age because no matter how wonderful parents and caregivers are, everyone always brings their own truth to the table. It is a human thing to do and usually not hurtful for children, but think how eager kids are to live and tell their own tales. This book presents a beautiful solution—to help children BE and live what they came here to experience. Their truth! You can read more about *conscious parenting* in my book **Parenting Through the Eyes of Lollipops**.

You filled your fake void and re-remembered your own root-story, which is now imprinted on your forehead and in your heart. That makes what comes next your *combining time*! Yeehaw!

Stack your new - it is new, because you changed quite a bit through this process - *you* that you are now onto your true story of being little, and way before, atop an adventure that you have newly discovered and are happy to tell. How wonderful is that!

I'll leave some extra pages for you to write about your new combination of who you really are—your own phenomenal story.

Look around and focus on all beauty. Soon enough, you will believe and know that Life IS indeed beautiful!

Jacqueline Pirtle

_____

_____

_____

_____

_____

_____

_____

_____

_____

_____

_____

_____

_____

_____

_____

_____

_____

A STAR IS SHINING HIGH-FOR-LIFE

Imagine yourself experiencing the ultimate mastery of living a beautiful life...

That is high-for-life!

Being high-for-life is a state of complete alignment. It means that you are being and living your physical time as truthful for you as you can, as fitting for you as you can, and with a constant ability to shift yourself to a more fitting essence of being you; the result being, you are expanding and calibrating further and further into who you really are, and came here to BE.

Energetically, it does not scratch your soul being a bit if you are not aligned, because your soul always feels good—leaving your physical you as the one that is hurting. To clarify, never will your energetic essence come and live with you in your un-alignment and un-truthful state. Instead, your soul simply waits until you come to your senses and re-join that more intelligent part of yourself that was happily resting in bliss and glamour all along.

You came here, into physicality, to change all the time!

Which is a perfect choice—since life's, yours, and the universe's natural state is also changing all the time. Keeping up with those changes means that you are in the flow with physical life, your soul being, and consciousness. There is no pressure, resistance, or unwell-ness in that flow, instead it is a beautiful state with the energetic value of peace, effortlessness, and in ease. Only when living against this natural flow of change, can resistance and pressure get entangled in life— unwell-feelings arise and become the experience that you live.

High-for-life living means that you adapt to these constant changes by allowing them to take root, by receiving them in peace, and by keeping up with your always being-new!

High-for-life alignment also means that:

• When you are sad and feel well in that sadness while dwelling and crying like a dog, you are in alignment—until it does not feel good anymore, which shifts you into disalignment.

• When you are angry and are feeling well in your anger - yes, you can actually feel amazing while angry - by boxing a pillow, not someone else, you are aligned, until it does not feel good anymore—shifting you into disalignment.

• When you are emotionally down and are happy that way, you are in alignment. Sometimes this presents a well-feeling excuse to binge-watch or eat plenty of comfort food, like ice cream. Use that excuse and feel okay in it until unwellness takes over—that is your cue to put the ice cream away, turn the episodes off, and go run and jump while eating salad instead, shifting you back into being in alignment.

High-for-life means that you care profoundly about how you feel, and are willing to align yourself with who you are right at this given moment—no matter what that looks like.

Enjoy this real-time you!

As long as you feel good you are aligned, and remember, you can always shift to something better when it gets old and moldy. That is the ultimate mastery of the art of living a beautiful life; that is high-for-life!

I invite you to ask yourself: How am I feeling right now? What would be a betterment for me right now? What does it mean for me to BE and live high-for-life? What essence represents me and my true alignment right now?

I couldn't resist leaving you a few pages to write about your high-for-life scenario. I say, "Ready, set, scribble!" Please play with the idea of getting yourself a journal, so you can continue to keep writing your phenomenal story once these pages are filled. And for a last time:

Important! These feelings are unique for everyone—it is supposed to be like that. That's why I am not going to say what they have to be, or the outcome that this journal entry must have. It might also take a few times until you really get the sense for this type of work, since it might not be the norm of what you have been practicing or been taught to do. This is not a one-time exercise—rather, it is meant to be performed many times, over and over as a journey, if you will. Some sensing might be of bliss right at the first try, while for others it might spark sadness, fear, anger, or old unwell-feelings at first. This is normal. It is also not unusual if today, it's pure bliss, and next time it's a sense of anything but bliss. That is okay too! Remember, you are cleansing out any untruth - fear, anger, sadness - to get to your core of your pure positive energy. Think of it like layers—your first time sensing, a layer of sadness might show itself; next time you sense, a layer of anger; next time, it is all bliss and you are at your core of being pure positive energy. Once that happens, experiencing this beautiful part of you will give you a sense of what you are feeling for, moving forward in your life—it's like a north star for you to focus on.

Keep an open mind and continue with your sensing in lighthearted-ness, awe, and joyful-ness. Whenever it will resonate, and whatever this brings forth for you, it is perfect, for you!

Your new beginning - your new story - will be written little by little every time you come back to this. Make it on *your* terms and base it on *when* and *how* it is best for you!

Look around and focus on all beauty. Soon enough, you will believe and know that Life IS indeed beautiful!

CLOSING THOUGHTS

Because I don't want the book to end. Instead, I want to talk about some real life-dookie examples and why they are beautiful...

So here it goes...

THE BEAUTY OF CRAZY-NESS

Beauty is when you give your own spirit permission to dance in harmony with the spirit of life...

Life is crazy, you are crazy, physicality is crazy—and would you want it any other way?

Imagine yourself hopping onto a ride at an amusement park. All excited and adventurous; in for the experience of fun, spontaneity, and craziness—not for being in control of the ride, which is on point since once you are on the ride you have literally no say in how this machine works. But isn't that what you were looking for, an adventure full of surprises?

Life is no different! You are invited to fully, and with your utmost trust, let go of everything that you have ever thought to be true or real. Instead, latch on to the wild energetic ride of your spiritual being - since your physical you is not, never was, and never will be in charge anyways - and enjoy the chaotic rules of this beautiful adventure called life.

You are in charge of how you feel, and have the capability to align with your terrific-ness—all else, let it go. Just imagine all the magic that can freely happen as such.

I say drop everything, close your eyes, and visualize yourself hopping on your own crazy energetic ride and let your spiritual part take over—just as this rollercoaster ride, if that is the ride you chose, took over.

Breathe into this accelerating feeling! Can you feel the shift - the change - of your energetic value that just happened for you? You are elevated, and so is every single cell of your whole being; body, mind, soul, and consciousness. This is now the precious worth that you will spread to everything and everyone—and all of consciousness.

It is so easy to get along with craziness. It is so easy to shift yourself from disliking chaos to trusting and loving it—energetically and then physically in life. Anyone can do it! No rocket science here.

Look around and focus on all beauty. Soon enough, you will believe and know that Life IS indeed beautiful!

THE BEAUTY OF PAIN

Pain and its many flavors belong to living a beautiful life...

Does that mean you want to create pain?

No, of course not! But you might as well embrace all the pain that you are experiencing and work its beauty, since it is here for you and will beautify your relationship with your whole being.

Pain on the physical level is your body talking to you. This type of language has incredible and intelligent information and if you chat with it you will understand its origin, its creation, its meaning, and its healing.

Emotional pain is very much the same. It is a guidance system for you to get to know yourself better, and to stand more aligned with your truth.

Here are the steps to celebrate the beauty of any pain:

• Acknowledge the pain for what it is—great intelligent wisdom.

• Accept, respect, appreciate, thank, and love it for what it is—a well-meaning clump of information about you and for you.

• Invite the pain to stay as long as it wants. Making space for your pain to BE means that you are making space for an important part of you to BE—and no slice of you wants to be wished into nonexistence!

• Start chatting away with it... Ask your pain what it is, where it is coming from, what it is telling you, and what you can do differently to calm and soothe it.

- Take beautiful action by following the guidance you receive—all while focusing on choosing, imagining, and living your next new reality of betterment. Show gratitude for your pain-free new existence!

This pain-respecting protocol shifts you and your pain into a beautiful relationship, which might even grow into a love-relationship. Your pain becomes a part of you, and instead of hating it, or wanting it to go away, you are allowing it to BE a beautiful sign—helping you to live a happy and healthy life.

Everything is an energetic essence, pain too, and can always be shifted into a different experience—by you!

Look around and focus on all beauty. Soon enough, you will believe and know that Life IS indeed beautiful!

NOT HERE TO ALWAYS PLAY IT SAFE, CALM, AND SECURE

Nobody ever chose anything else but to expand and calibrate into more bliss and joy when coming into this physical life...

When you constantly choose to feel better and more aligned with your pure bliss and joy, you let go of the non-realistic and not well-feeling focus to always stay safe, calm, and secure in life.

This is not to say that you don't want to be safe, calm, and secure—in situations like crossing the street focusing on safety is a must! So please, take care of yourself, because we are only talking about a shift in focus here.

To continue...

Many times bliss and joy is the same as being or feeling safe, calm, and secure—a wonderful, super aligned experience indeed.

But what about the times where bliss and joy matches up with you being wild and crazy—the opposite of safe, calm, and secure? If your main focus is and stays on being safe, calm, and secure, you won't be fulfilling your duty to align with your soul being that is rooting for wild and crazy—surpassing all opportunities to meet up with the perfect happenings in life.

Focusing on safe, calm, and secure, means that you go against life a lot of times—since you did not come here to focus on safety but rather on your alignment of well-feeling. This creates pressure and resistance, not to mention disalignment and lack of trust in life.

Aligning with your truth of being pure positive energy - happiness, joy, bliss, and well-feeling - is always the better choice than solely focusing on being safe, calm, secure, or any of those physical life preferences.

Plus, your constant process of aligning with your truth, your inner guidance, and your most accurate intelligence is making sure that you are safe, calm, and secure because it guides you exactly to where you want or need to be—and to all experiences that you are here to have in order to expand and calibrate further as you.

If in that alignment you are guided to safety, calmness, and security, you aligning with it will be of a well-feeling nature - no resistance or pressure will be present - and if your inner guidance tells you to go wild and crazy, following that hint will make sure that you are safe, calm, and secure while being in your alignment.

Look around and focus on all beauty. Soon enough, you will believe and know that Life IS indeed beautiful!

And that, my dear reader, is the end of this book. In truth I could have kept adding on to those last thoughts, making it the longest self-help book you have ever read, while probably putting you into a bored state at some point. To avoid that scenario and to keep the focus of this book on *Life IS Beautiful: Here's to New Beginnings*, I'll end it here, but know that my next book will be coming out soon...

I hope you enjoyed this book as much as I loved writing it. If you did, it would be wonderful if you could take a short minute and leave a review on Amazon.com and Goodreads.com as soon as you can, as your kind feedback is much appreciated and so very important. Thank you!

For any questions you might have and for more information on my sessions, workshops, presentations, and whatever else I am up to, visit my website www.freakyhealer.com and my social media accounts @freakyhealer.

Thank you again for enjoying and supporting my work. You mean the whole bar of chocolate to me.

Yours,

Jacqueline

Look around and focus on all beauty. Soon enough, you will believe and know that Life IS indeed beautiful!

ABOUT THE AUTHOR

Jacqueline Pirtle is the owner of the lifestyle company FreakyHealer. She is a holistic practitioner, a speaker, and a bestselling author. Her books, *365 Days of Happiness*, *Parenting Through the Eyes of Lollipops*, *What it Means to BE a Woman*, and *Life IS Beautiful* represent her passion for mindful happiness which shines through in all areas of her life and work helping clients to shift into a high-for-life frequency—a unique experience that calls people into their highest potential in their NOW!

Jacqueline has been featured in multiple online magazines, including Authority Magazine, Thrive Global, NBC NewsBetter, has appeared on Women Inspired TV, and interviewed on radio shows such as The Sunday School Radio Show, The Lisa Radio Show and WoMRadio. Her article "Are You Happy?" is in print in The Edge Magazine.

Jacqueline was born in Switzerland, has lived all over the world, and now makes her home in the US with her phenomenal family. Her professional background is in holistic wellness and natural living, she holds various international degrees, and is an internationally certified Reiki Master. She also considers herself a professional red wine and dark chocolate taster.

52835009R00095